AUTOMATIC PLEASURES

The History Of The
Coin Machine

Nic Costa

Published by Kevin Francis Publishing Limited

ACKNOWLEDGEMENTS

Frederick Bolland; Tom Boland; Harry Holloway; Jimmy Broderick; Dr. Seltenreich; Herb Jones; Dick Bueschel; Paul Haskell; Padraig Madden; Jon Gresham; John Hayward; Clive Baker; Brian Bates; Graham Brierley; Richard Haynes; Gaston Stiel; Jean-Claude Baudot; Guy Degrelle; Alan Osbourne; Bob Klepner; World's Fair UK; Coin Slot USA; British Library; British Patents Office; and last but not least, to my long suffering family: Pat, Gallia and Electra.

Cover by Chris Murdock, Jon Sayer.

Additional Copies
Further copies of this book can be obtained by ordering from Kevin Francis Publishing Ltd., Landcroft House, 85 Landcroft Road, East Dulwich, London SE22 9JS. Cheques/PO for £16.95 plus 75p p&p should be made payable to Kevin Francis Publishing. Overseas buyers should add £3 for p&p.

Any reader who wishes to contact the author for further information on coin machines should write via the publishers address.

First Edition
© Nic Costa 1988
Typeset by Greenwich Press, London
Printed in Great Britain by The Bath Press

Dedicated to Freddie Bolland

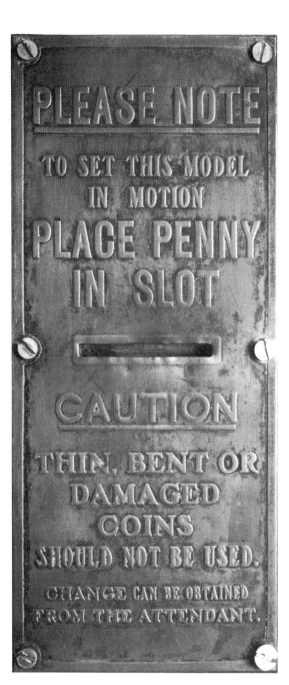

CONTENTS

The Automatic Revolution   7

Automatic Entertainment   21

Gambling Machines   35

The One Arm Bandit   49

Illicit Activities   63

Legitimisation   79

The Machines   93

Billiands and Pin Bagatelle   127

Competitive Games   137

Electric Shock Machines   145

Fortune Tellers   153

Music and Sound Machines   161

Shooting Games   169

Strength Testers   179

Vending and Service Machines   185

Viewers   193

Wall Machines   201

The Working Model   209

Appendix   217

Everitt's Automatic Postal Card Box 1883

CHAPTER ONE

The Automatic Revolution

It must come as a surprise to many to learn just how old coin operated devices are. Indeed, to find the first recorded instance of the use of them one has to travel back in time almost 2,000 years to the Hellenistic world of Alexandria in Egypt. When synthesised, the inventions of this civilisation were truly staggering, even by modern standards. As Morris Kline writes in his book, 'Mathematics in Western Culture':

> They designed improved water clocks and sundials and used them to good advantage in the courts to limit lawyers speeches. Pumps, pulleys, wedges, tackles, geared devices and a mileage measuring device no different from the ones to be found in the modern automobile were widely employed. Among the mechanical inventions were new instruments for astronomical measurements. To the mathematician and inventor Heron (first century B.C.), the age owed an automatic machine for sprinkling holy water when a five-drachma coin was inserted. Musical organs could be operated in a similar way. The temples mystified the public with doors that opened when the coins were deposited.
>
> A study of gases and liquids produced a water-driven organ, a gun powered by compressed air, and a hose for spraying liquid fire. The public gardens were enhanced by water fountains with moving statues driven by water pressure.
>
> The generation of steam power was another development of the Alexandrians. It was used to drive automobiles along the city streets in the annual religious parades. When produced by fires maintained under the temple altars, the steam put life into the gods. Awestruck audiences observed gods who shed tears, and statues that poured out libations. Mechanical doves rose up into the air and descended by means of the unobservable action of steam.

Unhappily, few if any of the more radical inventions were to elicit more than a passing interest. In a society which in the main regarded slavery as one of its fundamental tenets, and therefore saw little need for the use of machinery as a means of replacing manual labour, such inventions were seen as novelties and as mere novelties they were to remain.

The widespread application of the mechanical principles which provided the motive power for these early devices had to wait for centuries, until the development of a society which relied heavily upon the use of paid labour. The development of markets and 'paid labour' encouraged the introduction of devices designed to increase production and reduce costs.

Electrically operated chocolate dispenser

Weighing Machine with automatic indicator

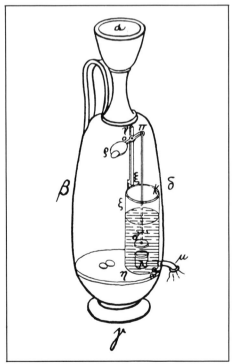

Hero's coin operated Holy Water dispenser

Coin operated Photomaton

The Industrial Revolution in 18th century Britain was to provide the first tentative beginnings of a new age, one which has increasingly relied upon the use of machinery as a means of supplementing or enhancing the production of goods or services. It was during this new age of innovation and invention that the coin freed machine was to reappear, at first making a negligible impact upon the course of daily life.

In its earliest form it was to be encountered in taverns and the like, as an Honour Box. As its name implies it relied heavily upon the user's honesty. It consisted in essence of a small portable box divided into two compartments, one to hold the coins and the other to hold a quantity of loose tobacco. Insertion of a coin would release a lever enabling the user to open the compartment containing the tobacco and he was then 'honour bound' to take only as much tobacco as he had paid for. As crude and simplistic as the device was, it was to survive in use until the middle of the 19th century.

London in the 1820s was to witness the introduction by Richard Carlisle, the famous radical bookseller, of a unique and curious device. Its primary function was to assist Carlisle in the sale of prohibited or proscribed literature, the sale of which had hitherto subjected Carlisle and his assistants to legal harassment. It took the form of a large coin freed book vending machine attached to the front of his shop. The names of the books vended were inscribed on a large dial. The purchaser would turn a pointer to the name of the book he wanted, insert his money and the appropriate volume would be delivered. However (and here lies the rub) on the other side of the 'machine' out of sight of the user would be an assistant waiting to take the money and place the appropriate volume into the chute.

The idea was to stop the purchaser identifying the seller, thereby forestalling a prosecution. Unfortunately the ploy was not a success as Carlisle found to his cost, when faced with yet another charge of selling seditious literature!

By the 1830s in Britain, more sophisticated versions of the Honour Boxes were to be encountered, which vended a predetermined amount of tobacco for a given coin. The tobacco would be wrapped in paper and stacked in a column. Access to the tobacco would be by means of a coin freed drawer.

At least one of these early devices has survived. It was manufactured and operated in New York in the 1840s, and was based upon an earlier British machine. However, the first coin freed patent per se was not applied for until 1857. In that year Simeon Denham of Wakefield in Yorkshire applied for a patent for 'A Self-Acting Machine for the Delivery of Postage And Receipt Stamps'. He was given provisional protection for his machine. It was designed to sell a stamp from a strip of postage stamps contained within it. A penny inserted would automatically feed out a stamp from the roll. That the machine was not a commercial success is attested to by the fact that Denham never bothered to take out a full patent for his invention.

The year 1867 was to witness two further patents. The first of these was granted in Britain for a fortune telling device designed to answer questions by means of the discs inserted into it. The second was granted in Germany for a vending machine designed to sell handkerchiefs, cigarettes and sweets.

TRYING POSITION OF AN ELDERLY GENTLEMAN.

He determines to try the Automatic Photographing Machine, the Station being empty. To his dismay a Crowd has gathered, and watches the Operation.

"At the Sign of the 'Budget Shop.'"

TRYING HER STRENGTH.

Madame La Republique. "Aha!—I have pulled 'im now—at last!!"

"A LIBERAL MEASURE."

Rude Boy (to Stout Party on Weighing-Machine, which is out of order, and won't work). "Shove in another Penny, Guv'ner. It's Double Fare to Chaps o' your size!"

Selection of real machines featured in Punch cartoons of the 1890's

10

Over the course of the next 15 years Britain was to witness the granting of a total of 12 patent applications for coin freed devices. By the start of 1883 the prospective purchaser could (if he could find the machines) buy: stamps, photographs or almanacs; any number of other small articles (notably cigarettes); obtain change for his gold sovereign; enter through an automatic turnstile; close the toilet door; play a game of billiards or bagatelle; tell his fortune and if this wasn't enough (although Patent Office records remain silent) insert a penny to see a model working, sometimes to a musical accompaniment.

The efforts of the early coin machine makers were to be the tentative foundations upon which future dreams and empires would be built. All of them applied for only one coin freed patent, indicating that they were not successful in their ambitions. The year 1883 was to prove the turning point. From then on there was was an enormous increase in the number of patent applications (3 in 1883, 6 in 1884, 20 in 1885, 70 in 1886, 139 in 1887 etc.), so much so that by the mid 1890s an excess of 1,000 patent applications for coin freed machines had been received by the U.K. Patents Office.

The introduction of coin freed machines during the last quarter of the 19th century was symptomatic of the radical changes that were taking place in Western society during this period. It was a time when so many of the things that we now consider a vital part of our daily lives were first developed or introduced, not as accidents of history, but as tangible realities. Inextricably linked to the advent of these new technologies were the changes within Western society itself. There were new laws on public health, education, housing and factories; there was increased mechanisation; the growth of new industrial towns and cities; the introduction of the 5½ day working week; Bank Holidays (from 1871); and a new and affluent middle class.

It is within this context therefore that one must seek to explain the introduction and subsequent proliferation of coin operated machines on a mass scale during the last quarter of the 19th century.

An Automatic World
By 1890 the satirical magazine Punch (tongue as ever firmly in cheek) saw fit to comment upon the situation in an article entitled: "The Way We Shall Live Soon . . . (From the Diary of the Automatically Conducted)." It went as follows:

> 7 A.M. turned out of automatically constructed bed and deposited on the floor. Am picked up and hurled into an automatic dressing, washing, and shaving chair, after which, being dressed by self-acting machinery, descend by switch-back lift to dining room, where I am fed by an 'automatic private breakfast supplier' while listening to last night's speeches in the House, and the latest gossip, furnished by one of the 'Phonographic Association's Parliamentary and Social Scandal Machines.'

10 A.M. Take automatic horse exercise, and am thrown twice, being picked up each time automatically by a self-registering and revolving automatic policeman.

NOON — Attend the marriage of a favourite niece, assisting at the subsequent social entertainment which is supplied to the assembled guests on the platform of a West-End terminus from one of the 'Twopenny Wedding Breakfast Company's Automatic Machines,' the Bridegroom at the same time presenting the Bridesmaids with a handsome Penny Piece of Jewellery from a similar source.

4 P.M. Hair cut automatically, but, owing to some want of nice adjustment in the machinery, having managed to get ears clipped smartly at the same time, put penny into slot and consult an automatic pillar-post. Eventually get my head (and my hat too, by mistake) strapped up by patent automatic binder in the ward of an automatically conducted Hospital.

8 P.M. Dine automatically with automatic halfpenny appetite, listening to Phonographic Italian Opera at one of the Metropolitan District Underground Stations.

10 P.M. Dragged up-stairs mechanically by switch-back lift, and have my boots pulled off by machinery, being automatically flung into hot bath, turned out, scrubbed, lifted out, dried by a revolving towel, and eventually thrown into bed and tucked up, and finally sent to sleep by phonograph repeating good things said by funny man at previous day's evening-party

Everitt's Postcard Vender

As we have already noted, the year 1883 was to prove the turning point, for in April of that year one encounters a name which during the ensuing decade was to be often repeated in coin freed applications, not only in Britain, but across the world. The name is that of Percival Everitt. Sounding more like a secondary character from a Sherlock Holmes story, his genius was to lead, within the space of a few short years, to the establishment of an entire new industry, employing thousands of people, and generating an annual turnover, which in today's currency would amount to millions of pounds.

For his opening gambit Everitt, and his co-patentee J.G.Sandeman, were to market what at first sight would appear to be an exeedingly mundane device: a post-card vender. It was perhaps the very urbane nature of the machine that ensured its success, for by means of it Everitt was to tap into a new and very lucrative market. Postcards had first come into use in Austria in 1869 and by the mid 1870s they had been adopted as a convenient means of communication in many countries. In 1875 the General Postal Union was formed, leading directly to the international standardisation of size and postal rates applicable to the post-card. It was to prove big business, for by 1899 something in excess of 122 million post cards were being produced annually in Western Europe alone.

Although the machine was successful, there were difficulties, as evidenced by Everitt's 1885 patent for an improved version of his machine:

> It has been found in practice that although the apparatus is perfectly successful when not designedly misused, articles such as pieces of paper, orange peel and other rubbish have been maliciously placed in the slit provided for the admission of the coin, and that in consequence the channel provided for the passage of the coins from the slit became blocked, so that if a coin was subsequently inserted in the slit the apparatus would not act and the person attempting to use the apparatus could not obtain the postcard or other article for which he had paid by inserting a proper coin in the slit of the apparatus. It has also been found that by maliciously manipulating the delivery slide (in a manner which it is not necessary or expedient to state) it is occasionally possible. . to obtain more than one article.

How many times over the ensuing decades were these words to be echoed by despairing manufacturers and operators across the world! Despite these difficulties, which were never to be adequately solved during Everitt's lifetime, the enterprise was to meet with considerable success.

Following the introduction of Everitt's improved machine, both La Nature in France, and the Scientific American in the States were to write about it:

> It would be a great public convenience if each of us had at his disposal, away from home, night and day, at all hours and everywhere, postal cards, and stamped envelopes containing a sheet of letter paper. In fact it would be expedient to render depositories of these objects as numerous as letter boxes, but we cannot think of obtaining the multiplicity desirable by means of deliveries that are always open, since the expense of location, help, light, etc. would be out of all proportion to the income derived therefrom.
>
> Messrs Sandeman and Everitt have very happily solved the problem through an automatic distribution, their apparatus requiring the presence of 20 employees to manoeuvre it. One or two visits per day are sufficient for keeping the distributer full; the rest is an affair of the public. The arrangement which is shown in the engraving, is called the "Postal Card and Stamped Envelope Public Supply."
>
> The apparatus consists of a cast iron box 18 inches long, 12 inches wide, and 14 inches high, having a sloping cover upon which the writing may be done. Behind it there is a frame that contains a package of postal cards, and beneath the latter there is a drawer whose cavity is capable of containing one card, and one only. These cards are a little thicker than ordinary postal cards. The drawer, through a suitable mechanism, remains closed, and cannot be drawn

["A machine for amputation is being installed at the Emergency Hospital at Boston."—*Daily Mail.*]

THE AUTOMATIC DENTIST WILL NO DOUBT FOLLOW THE AMPUTATION MACHINE.

Of course, the "Automatic Conscience Clearer" for minor offences would soon be immensely popular. We beg to offer the above suggestion. N.B.—The Inventor has been provisionally protected.

Some additions we may reasonably expect to the Hot-water Lamp-posts.

AUTOMATIC ARBITRATION.

Selection of imaginery machines featured in Punch cartoons of the 1890's

out; but if a penny be dropped through a slit in the cover, it becomes unfastened, and, as it is pulled out, brings with it a postal card — the last one at the bottom of the package. When the drawer is shoved back it becomes locked again, and is ready to deliver another card upon the deposit of another coin, and so on, until the cards are exhausted. At this moment, through the removal of the last card, a spring closes the slit, so that a person cannot drop in any more coins, and at the same time displaying the inscription "EMPTY" thus giving the reason for the obstruction. In a compartment to the right is the package of stamped envelopes. This is manoeuvered in exactly the same way that the other is, but instead of one slot for one penny, there are two slits for a penny each. When the money box on either side has received its cash, the mechanism closes the slits until the goods paid for have been removed.

This apparatus is placed in all the railway stations of London and is so arranged as to be under the eye of the station employees. Although the slits permit the introducing of coins of definite dimensions only, and the mechanism works only under the action of a given weight, cases have occurred when certain unscrupulous and very ingenious persons have put pieces of lead of exactly the weight of a penny into the box; but such cases have been very rare.

Moreover, the risk is not much, since each compartment contains but 25 cards or envelopes. It would be easy, were it needed, to add an automatic electric bell, the ringing of which by attracting the attention of passers-by, would trouble guilty consciences. The box costs about thirty dollars. There are nearly a hundred placed in the London stations and cafes. They have proved a great success, both from the standpoints of curiosity and utility. In England all places are closed on Sunday, and the only way to get a postal card or stamped envelope is to have recourse to the supply box. We should not be surprised to see this ingenious vendor before long supplying small objects of regular prices and dimensions such as boxes of matches, cigars, omnibus tickets, etc!

Indeed, the writer of the article was not to be surprised. Between 1883 and 1891 Percival Everitt obtained no less than twenty-four coin freed patents covering a very wide range of machines. Between the years 1885-8 he was instrumental in the formation of at least five major companies, active on both sides of the Atlantic.

The Sweetmeat Automatic Delivery Company — A New Enterprise
The success of one of these companies was to be truly phenomenal. The Sweetmeat Automatic Delivery Company was registered as a limited company in November 1887 with a share capital of £100,000 (the original Post Card Supply Company founded in 1885 had a capital of £21,000). From the outset the company had some 1,500 machines in operation, the number of which was to grow fairly rapidly.

Based in London, it soon opened offices in Birmingham and Manchester, and it signed service contracts with 31 different supply companies. The list of articles vended through its machines was quite diverse, including; quinine, chocolate, cigars, cigarettes, chewing gum, matches, scent, biscuits, and even ants eggs! By 1901 the company had established its own sweet manufacturing plant in Glasgow. It operated machines on almost every railway station in the country (some 7000, in all). The company introduced such notable machines as the nameplate stamper, but went much further than one might expect, with an insurance policy vender which insured the buyer against accident for up to £100.

But railway stations, were not the only sites for SADC machines; amusement arcades, public houses, hotels, restaurants and shops also had them. One chain of London stores alone could boast 900 machines operated and serviced by the company.

Possibly the best indicator of the company's success was its share capital. In 1901 it was raised to almost £1.5 million, a sizeable amount at a time when a railway worker could expect to earn something like £60 a year!

An Inundation of Automatons
Everitt had been joined by literally hundreds of inventors (and investors) across Western Europe and North America, each seeking to stake their claim to a share of the 'automatics goldmine'. In 1895 De Natuur wrote:

> At the present time we are being inundated with automatons. If this continues, the time will come when all the arts and crafts will be performed by machines which, at the cost of a coin, be it large or small, will be at everybody's service. At this point, human hands will be necessary only for producing the automatons, unless of course automatons are invented which are capable of performing

Automatic Bar: Societe Francaise des Fontaines Populaires 1890

this work too. One cannot enter a public place nowadays without seeing a weighing-machine, a chocolate machine and frequently, a penny-in-the- slot machine rendering some popular waltz at the cost of a copper or two. At the World Exhibition now being held in Amsterdam, these ingenious machines are present in a wide variety of shapes and forms, each more ingenious than the last. There are automatons for beverages dispensing refreshments for a few coins, hens laying tin eggs filled with sweets and as befits a chicken, cackling loudly as the eggs emerge to announce that they are on the way. There are dainty automatic misses who offer you a choice of chocolates on a tray after you have sacrificed a penny, but the chief object of admiration is the slot machine that produces within the brief space of three minutes a tolerable likeness of whoever cares to pay a shilling for his portrait.

From 1883 until the turn of the century there were to be many 'firsts' in the field of automatic machines and some of them were to play a key role in society. They not only introduced new technologies to the public at large but also became an integral part of everyday life. The following is a list, though by no means exhaustive, of these items:

1884 Telephone. The telephone had been invented just eight years earlier in America by Alexander Graham Bell.
The ticket dispensing weighing machine. Patented by Everitt, this machine was to be heavily marketed on both sides of the Atlantic.

1885 Strength Tester
Liquid dispenser

1886 Electric shock machine
Lung tester
Stereo viewer
Height measurer
Hot drinks vender

1887 Electric light. The first coin operated electric light was designed for use in hotels, railway carriages etc. Crucial to this was the light bulb, invented in 1878 it was not manufactured on a mass scale until 1881.
Gas meter. Crucial to the use of gas in the home, initially as a means of lighting was the gas mantle, invented in 1885.
Horse racer
Shooter
Speed tester
Photographic machine. This machine automatically took, developed, and delivered a photograph of the user. It was made possible by the development of gelatin dry plates in 1878, which were much more sensitive to light and required a much shorter exposure time.

Phonograph. Initially combined with other coin operated devices so as to make talking weighing machines, talking vending etc. The first phonograph had been invented by Thomas Alva Edison some ten years earlier.

1888 Opera glasses
Sight tester
Savings bank. This allowed money to be deposited in a bank in exchange for a receipt.

1889 Age calculator
Ticket machine for railways and trams
Phrenological machine
Spinning pointer/dial machine for use as a fortune teller or gambling game.

1890 Caretaker for property
Towel machine

1891 Lift. The first electically operated lifts were introduced in 1889.
Boot cleaner
Telegraph

1892 Toilet paper

1893 Telescope
Kinetoscope. Effectively the first 'living picture' machine, the direct precursor of the cinema. Invented by W K L Dickson and Thomas Alva Edison.
Two player competitive game.

1895 Mutoscope

1897 X-ray machine. These were marketed following the discovery by Konrad Rontgen of X-rays in 1895.

1898 Compressed air machine. Used for pumping up the tyres of bicycles automobiles, etc. The pneumatic tyre had been re-invented in 1888.

1899 Automatic restaurant.

By far the greatest number of patents granted during this period related to vending machines; machines which either provided a service, or sold items of every day necessity. Radical changes in society were expected as a direct result of their introduction. Fears were expressed on a number of occasions that the widespread use of such devices would lead to wholesale redundancy, particularly in the retail and catering service.

Such fears were to prove unfounded. The dream of the inventors had in fact surpassed their society's technical ability to make such a dream manifest.

Much of the innovator's fervour was to provide but a transitory vision of today's technology. Yet the whole of the early revolution rested upon the solution to one fundamental problem — how to make a coin slot which not only operated the mechanism, but also resisted all attempts on the part of the public to defraud it. In an honest society this would not have been a problem, but in the real world (as we have already noted in the Everitt patent extract) there is no such thing as an honest society. In the real world, the coin entry mechanism had to cope with all sorts of abuse — pieces of paper, sticky sweets, buttons, washers, thumping and still remain sensitive enough to operate upon the insertion of a coin. It was a problem which was to elude adequate solution for many decades.

The earliest recorded case relating to theft from a coin machine, in Britain, dates back to 1887, when three young men were convicted of larceny for using brass discs to obtain cigars. At times, the attitude of the authorities could be quite nebulous, as is revealed, for example, in this extract from an 1891 copy of the 'Illustrated American'.

> Recently a magistrate of St Louis was was called upon to decide a very curious case. A policeman on his beat was attracted by shouts of delight raised by a crowd of spectators in a public thoroughfare. Drawing nearer, he discovered the centre of attraction was a gentleman who was manipulating a slot machine that dispensed cigars. He had punched a hole through a nickel and there he stood dropping the nickel into the slot and drawing it out again and every time he did so a cigar fell out of the receptacle. This ingenious gentleman had secured 25 cigars when arrested. He was generous withal for he was distributing them around the crowd. The latter followed him to the magistrates office and here the complicated question arose as to whether the offence was larceny. The magistrate gave it up and compromised by fining the man $5 for disorderly conduct on the streets.

The problem of inefficient and unreliable coin entry mechanisms inevitably consigned many of the more grandiose schemes to early oblivion. Indeed, as early as the first half of the 1890s, when the coin machine boom was in full swing and a fully automated society seemed just around the corner, staid business journals were busy warning off prospective investors from sinking their money into automatic concerns. As a consequence vending machines tended to develop in the following decades primarily as purveyors of cheap everyday items such as matches, cigarettes, or chewing gum, whilst their more ambitious counterparts, such as gold sovereign changers, and fully automatic restaurants and public houses faded from the scene.

However, the lack of an efficient coin entry mechanism was not to hamper the development of other types of machine, especially in cases where the user was offered no tangible return for his money — the amusement and gambling machines!

Ally Sloper vending machine: Interchangeable Company, London c1899

CHAPTER TWO

Automatic Entertainment

The 1880s and 90s were, as we have seen, a boom period of automatic invention throughout the whole of Western Europe and North America. Almost all the types of coin operated machine with which we are now familiar have their origins during this period.

Central to the popularisation of automatic machines in the early years were the various railway companies, which from the late 1870s onwards adorned their stations with a wide variety of coin operated machines. Although the emphasis was to be primarily upon vending or service machines they were also responsible for the development of 'arcade' machines.

Perhaps the earliest type of this class of machine to be encountered was the **working model**, a stationary object (usually a railway engine or a steam ship) in a glass case which came to life at the insertion of a penny. It often served a dual purpose, for it not only gave the user 'amusement' but also advertised various travel companies.

Such models in more macabre or moral form were to remain the mainstay of the amusement business throughout the first half of the 20th century, particularly in Britain.

Fortune tellers were also amongst the earliest types of this class of machine to be exploited at railway stations. It was essentially from these that many of the gambling games were to draw their inspiration (indeed, many of the early patents bear witness to this, by stating that such machines could be used either as fortune tellers, or in modified form as games of chance). A person could discover his future by means of a spinning pointer, dial, reel, card dispenser, or more exotically through the medium of an animated figure.

Athletic machines were also very popular. They were capable of measuring almost every aspect of a persons strength, from his grip, punch, or kick, although a misplaced blow could ocasionally result in an unconscious customer or a broken hand. Popular too were the **health machines** which would tell a person his height, his weight, the condition of his lungs or even give him an electric shock — then a recommended remedy for numerous ailments. Competitive machines enabled players to pit their skills against each other, whilst **shooting games** enabled players to fulfil their patriotic duty by heeding Lord Salisbury's dictum that 'Every man should learn to shoot!' **Music machines** including disc phonographs, were the ancestors of the modern juke box and they would play all the latest tunes. **Stereo, Flip-Card,** or real **Film Machines** gave the user visual access not only to world events but also a butler's eye view through the keyhole!

Kinetoscope 1894

The Birth of the Cinema

The concept of an entirely automated establishment occured early on. It had been put into practice in Paris, for example, in 1890 where the Societe Francais des Fontaines Populaires were operating an entirely automatic bar. Customers could, for the insertion of an appropriate coin, obtain spirits beer or coffee.

In America in the summer of 1892, Edison and his associates decided that the Kinetoscope should be marketed in much the same way. The first Kinetoscope parlour opened in New York in the 14th April 1894. Although it was operated by means of a ticket system, it was to prove the exception rather than the rule, as most of the subsequent parlours were to use coin operated versions of the same machine. It was an immediate success, as evidenced by the following account given by Alfred Tate:

> We then decided to install ten of these (i.e. Kinetoscopes) in New York . . . and in preparation for this I leased a small store, formerly a shoe shop, No 1155 Broadway, in the west side near Twenty-seventh Street . . . Here the ten machines were placed in the center of the room in two rows of five each, enclosed by a metal railing for the spectators to lean against when viewing the animated picture. One ticket, at the price of twenty five cents, entitled the holder to view one row of five machines. If he wanted to see both rows he bought two tickets. On the right of the entrance door a ticket booth was erected. At the back of the exhibition room was a smaller room

for use as an office and for repairing the films. In the window there was a printed announcement or advertisment whose legend I cannot now recall, and a plaster bust of Edison painted to simulate bronze. It was an exellent portrait but a few weeks later I received a message from Edison asking me to remove it. He thought its display undignified.

By noon on Saturday, the 14th of April, 1894, everything was ready for the opening of the exhibit to the public on the following Monday. My brother, the late Bertram M. Tate, was to act as manager; a mechanic was to supervise the machines, and an attractive young woman was to preside over the ticket booth. Both were to report for duty at nine o'clock in the morning of that day. At one o'clock on this notable Saturday afternoon, after locking the street door, Lombard, my brother and I went to Lunch. Returning at two o'clock, I locked the door on the inside and we all retired to the office in the rear to smoke and engage in general conversation. We had planned to have an especially elaborate dinner at Delmonico's then flourishing at the south east corner of Broadway and Twenty-sixth Street, to celebrate the initiation of the Kinetoscope enterprise. From where I sat I could see at the display window the groups who stopped to gaze at the bust of Edison. A brilliant idea occured to me.

"Look here," I said, pointing towards the window, " Why shouldn't we make that crowd out there pay for our dinner tonight?"

They both looked and observed the group before the window as it dissolved and renewed itself.

"What's your scheme?" asked Lombard with a grin.

"Bert," I said to my brother, "you can stand near the door and act as a reception committee. We can run till six o'clock and by that time we ought to have dinner money."

We all thought it a good joke. Lombard stationed himself at the head of the row of machines, my brother stood ready to supervise them, and I unlocked and opened the door and then entered the ticket booth where printed tickets like those now in use were ready to be passed out. And then the procession started.

I wish now that I had recorded the name of the person to whom I sold the first tickets. It was a good joke alright, but the joke was on us. If we had wanted to close the place at six o'clock it would have been necessary to engage a squad of policemen. We got no dinner. At one o'clock in the morning I locked the door and we went to an all- night restaurant to regale ourselves on broiled lobsters, enriched by the sum of about one hundred and twenty dollars.

Before the year was out the Kinetoscope was to be found in every major city on both sides of the Atlantic as entrepreneurs rushed in to take a slice of the action. By December 1894, just eight months after the initial New York opening there were something in excess of 80 Kinetoscope parlours

Lion Jawed Man

Tattooed couple at tea

A fat lady

24

or exhibitions in operation. In October of that year the first Kinetoscope parlour was opened in London by the Continental Commerce Company (set up to exploit the Kinetoscope in Europe). They were soon to have stiff competition not only from machines imported direct from the United States but also copies of the original machine (made in London by Robert Paul). So much so, that before a month had passed, London could boast five such establishments. (Edison's lack of foresight meant that he had neglected to patent the machine in Europe, thereby allowing competitors to produce copies of it without fear of prosecution.)

However, the Kinetoscope boom, for all its initial vigour, was to be relatively short lived. By 1900 production of the machine had all but ceased, developments in film projection led in their turn to the establishment of permanently sited cinemas by the early 1900s.

The Travelling Showman
Synchronous with the appearance of the Kinetoscope was the exploitation of other coin operated devices by travelling showmen. The travelling showman as a breed had existed for centuries, seeking to earn a living by exhibiting the latest novelty, spectacle, or technological wonder. The showman was essentially an itinerant traveller earning a living as best he could in any number of ways, both legal and illegal. An English writer at the turn of the century provides us with an insight into his activities:

> There is one of this latter class (of shooting gallery) at Islington; it is a fixture there all year round, and at the right time of year the proprieter enlarges his enterprise by engaging travelling showmen to set up their shows in his first floor apartments. The right time of year is the winter. Throughout the summer they tour about in caravans and are to be viewed in tents at country fairs; but winter drives them into London and the big provincial cities. Here their showmen sometimes hire untenanted shops at low rentals till they are re-let, and run shows on their own account. Oftener they are glad to get engagements for successive weeks at regular show places, such as the two at Islington, those in Whitechapel, in Kilburn, in Deptford, or in Canning Town.
>
> Wherefore, while the Cattle Show and later the World's Fair are in progress at the Agricultural Hall, you may pay your penny and be entertained over the shooting gallery at Islington by a pair of Oriental jugglers in one room, and in the other by a gentleman and his wife who are tattooed from necks to heels with ingenious designs in half the colours of the rainbow. Going again next week you will find the front room appropriated to an elegant 'electric lady', who communiciates electric shock to those who touch her; while the back room is the happy hunting ground of the noble savage . . .
>
> During this same period the Whitechapel establishment is graced by the presence of a fat woman of stupendous girth and weight. Here the shows are held in the shop itself, the rearward half of it being temporarily curtained off just now and transformed into a

living room for the stout lady, she taking no pleasure in going up and down stairs . . . Next week she is bewitching Islington; the tattooed people have transferred themselves to Canning Town; and the noble savage is earning fresh laurels with his tankard in the wilds of Kilburn.

Waxworks Shooting Galleries and Freaks

These were some of the more traditional pursuits of the showman. Others with more money or artistic flair did not have to exhibit themselves, but could procure freaks of nature, which came ready pickled in glass jars for the delectation of the paying public.

One of the most popular of all shows was the waxworks exhibition, some of which travelled the country, while others established themselves at permanent locations. Again, we are able to take a peek at a turn of the century waxworks exhibition:

> The window tempting you with a waxwork nurse soothing a wounded waxwork soldier by showing him a bottle of physic, you pay at the turnstile in the doorway, the lady attendant discontinuing a fantasia on the barrel organ to take your penny. The shop and the floors above are rich in waxen allegories symbolising the might of the British Empire; also in wax, models of statesmen, warriors, thinkers, with here and there distributed among them renowned ruffians who have been crowded out of the Chamber of horrors, which galaxy of great criminals is on the third floor here, though in some of the other waxworks it is down in the basement and gains an additional horror from its situation. The chief object in the principal room is a waxwork Cabinet Meeting, obviously called together at a supreme crisis, for three ministers have risen to speak simultaneously and a choice collection of British generals is crowded into a tight corner in the immediate background for any emergency. You may not recognise everybody, but that is immaterial, as each gentleman has his name written on a scrap of paper pinned to his chest.

Mention has already been made of yet another extremely popular type of show; the shooting gallery. Shooting galleries were to be found in almost every part of London, either as permanent or seasonal fixtures. Sometimes they could be found in what to our eyes must seem the most unexpected of places.

Who today can imagine going into a hairdressers (or even a cutler's, if such places still existed) and finding therein a shooting gallery which used, more often than not, live ammunition?

The scenes we have glimpsed of the showman's life could have been witnessed in almost any year of Queen Victoria's venerable reign. In the main, they were presenting shows and attractions which had their origins in the distant past and which had proved perennially popular. The rapid rise to prominence of the coin operated machine in the late 1880s and early

1890s by virtue not only of its novelty but also of its diversity of form and function posed such a direct threat to the livelihood of the showman, that he either had to accept it with open arms, or go under.

Evidence of this is furnished by our contemporary observer:

> This 'slot' variety is a recent development, and managers of the older sideshows find it such a formidable competitor that they adopt it now as a supplement to their customary exhibits; hence the pleasure seeker is tempted in some busy London thoroughfare by a display of automatic picture machines ranged round an open-fronted shop, at the rear of which a shooting range yawns like a gigantic baker's oven, with gas jets shining in the depths of it; while for a penny paid to a vociferous showman he can go upstairs and admire a bearded lady seated in an otherwise empty drawing room, and look into the unfurnished dining room where, for his delight, three reputed Africans lick red-hot pokers that sizzle on their tongues, and quaff boiling lead out of rusty ladles with manifestations of keen enjoyment.

Indeed a quota of coin operated machines was indispensible at this time, and almost every show worth its salt in the late 1890s had to include them, be it a waxworks exhibition or a fat ladies convention!

Automatic Shops

From the mid-1890s onward, entire 'shops' were established, devoted solely to coin operated machines. Our Victorian observer wrote:

> Shops devoted wholly to automatic shows have multiplied rapidly, and are as popular in Blackwall, Kentish Town and Lambeth, as in Oxford Street and the more select ways of the West. Some drape their doors with crimson hangings and are ornately decorated inside, others are unadorned to very bleakness; but it is a rare thing to see any of them without visitors, and of an evening they are all crowded. The public enter gratis and, sooner or later, succumb to the fascinations of one or other of the machines, and drop in a penny or a halfpenny as the case may be, to set little leaden figures under glass playing cricket or football, or peer down a glazed opening and turn a handle to witness a scene from a familiar melodrama, the changing of the guard at Buckingham Palace, or some ludicrous episode of domestic life!

The writer goes on to give us yet another peek into one of these early arcades:

> It is a frontless shop in which well dressed people stroll among groves of automatic machines; at intervals a coin rattles into a slot and the whirr of the handle turning breaks the silence of the place, or the sharp crack of a rifle sounds, from the select shooting gallery

West End Sideshow c1900

at the end, where a marksman is disbursing a penny on two shots at the target!

Indeed it was in 'shops' like these, to be found by the late 1890s in all the major western cities, that many future business magnates were to be found, as hesitant young men dreaming of bright futures. Some were destined to earn fortunes in their chosen career, whilst others were to become rulers of the vast empires created by the burgeoning film and phonograph industries which they spawned. The 'automatic shop' had arrived and, in its most popular form, as the amusement arcade it was to become an integral part of daily life (in much the same way as the cinema). It has remained one of the prime outlets for the automatic machine during the course of the 20th century.

The Penny Arcade
Indeed, the early years of the 20th century were to be, if anything, the golden ones for the arcade. London alone in the early 1900s could boast something in excess of 170 such establishments, the same was to be true of all the major western cities. Herbert Mills, owner of the by now burgeoning Mills Novelty Company of Chicago was to write an appraisal of the business in one of the many promotional booklets produced by the company. It provides us with a unique insight into the nature of the arcade business at that time:

I have been in the amusement machine business for fifteen years and have made amusement machines of every description, but today I am concentrating my efforts upon one kind of machine, and that is the sort suitable for Automatic Vaudeville or Penny Arcades, as they are sometimes called. I have by my own personal example and effort raised the Arcade business from what it was to what it is today — a dignified, respectacle, highly profitable business, worthy of the effort and attention of any up-to-date progressive business man. The Arcade is no longer an experiment. In some states almost every town of 5,000 population or over has a permanent and successful Penny Arcade . . .

The Penny Arcade has become a permanent institution as much as the theatre, the opera, the circus, the concert, the lecture, or the gymnasium, for it combines in a modified form all of these and because it makes such universal appeal, particularly to the poorer classes, it is destined to grow constantly in popularity and size. Only about 10 per cent of the total population have an income of more than $1,200.00 per year and therefore, the percentage of those who can afford to pay a dollar for a concert ticket or two dollars for a theatre ticket is very small. But everyone can patronize the Penny Vaudeville and afford ten cents for half an hour's entertainment.

Let us see, for example, some of the things you can get for this sum. You can hear the finest music rendered by bands of noted musicians and listen to the voice of Caruso or Melba and hear them as distinctly as if paying instead of one cent, five dollars for an opera ticket. You can be transported in an instant as it were to many interesting spots thousands of miles away and can look at scenes which it would cost hundreds of dollars to reach by travel. You can engage in various athletic pastimes and use gymnasium apparatus, which would cost hundreds of dollars in your own home. The Penny Arcade, as it exists today, is an educator as much as the drama, the lecture or the museum . . .

Rifle Range, Islington c1900

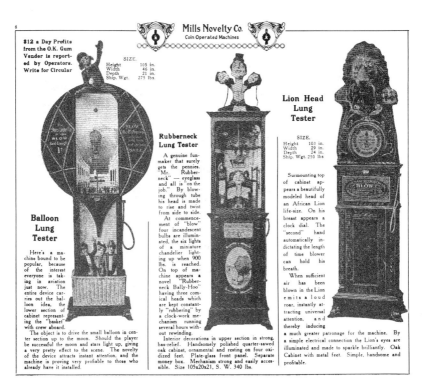

$12 a Day Profits from the O.K. Gum Vender is reported by Operators. Write for Circular

SIZE.
Height 105 in.
Width 46 in.
Depth 21 in.
Ship. Wgt. 275 lbs.

Lion Head Lung Tester

SIZE.
Height 103 in.
Width 29 in.
Depth 24 in.
Ship. Wgt. 250 lbs.

Rubberneck Lung Tester

A genuine fun-maker that surely gets the pennies. "Mr. Rubberneck" — eyeglass and all is "on the job." By blowing through tube his head is made to rise and twist from side to side.

At commencement of "blow" four incandescent bulbs are illuminated, the six lights of a miniature chandelier lighting up when 900 lbs. is reached. On top of machine appears a novel "Rubberneck Bally-Hoo" having three comical heads which are kept constantly "rubbering" by a clock-work mechanism running several hours without rewinding.

Interior decorations in upper section in strong, bas-relief. Handsomely polished quarter-sawed oak cabinet, ornamental and resting on four oxidized feet. Plate-glass front panel. Separate money box. Mechanism strong and easily accessible. Size 105x20x21, S. W. 340 lbs.

Surmounting top of cabinet appears a beautifully modeled head of an African Lion life-size. On his breast appears a clock dial. The "second" hand automatically indicating the length of time blower can hold his breath.

When sufficient air has been blown in the Lion emits a loud roar, instantly attracting universal attention, and thereby inducing a much greater patronage for the machine. By a simple electrical connection the Lion's eyes are illuminated and made to sparkle brilliantly. Oak Cabinet with metal feet. Simple, handsome and profitable.

Balloon Lung Tester

Here's a machine bound to be popular, because of the interest everyone is taking in aviation just now. The entire device carries out the balloon idea, the lower section of cabinet representing the "basket" with crew aboard.

The object is to drive the small balloon in center section up to the moon. Should the player be successful the moon and stars light up, giving a very pretty effect to the scene. The novelty of the device attracts instant attention, and the machine is proving very profitable to those who already have it installed.

Verbal Fortune Teller

Sibille Fortune Teller

Verbal Fortune Teller

" Wonderful Talking " Machine.
Actually Answers Questions.
Astonishes All Beholders.
Draws a Heavy Play.

Our very handsomest fortune teller—a really beautiful and remarkably clever machine and the only device of the kind which actually "speaks" the prophesies.

The highly polished cabinet is carved to represent the front of a Romany Gypsy Cart. In the interior hung with rich Oriental draperies and softly illuminated with art glass lantern, sits the veiled Mystic beautifully garbed. When coin is deposited she slowly turns her head, moves tongue, rolls her eyes and speaks aloud the fortune in a clear feminine voice. The amazing life-likeness of her actions holds patrons spellbound, and there is invariably an awe-struck crowd around the machine.

Explanation. Two phonographs are concealed in the lower sections of cabinet. The records each contain eleven appropriate fortunes for, respectively, men and women. The dropping of coin sets in action mechanism controlling action of head, eyes and tongue, and starts phonograph.

The machine is equipped with our famous New Automatic Transmission Spring Speed Regulator and Automatic Return Device. Wired to operate with either direct or alternating electric current and provided with wheels to facilitate moving about. Made for either nickels or pennies. A truly magnificent machine.

Famous Sibille Fortune Teller

One of the most attractive fortune tellers obtainable. In the upper section of the cabinet richly carpeted and hung with Oriental draperies sits Sibille—Queen of Hearts, attired in the luxurious garments of the East. From a jeweled diadem fall filmy veils of gauze half concealing her face and form. The whole softly illuminated by colored incandescent bulbs.

As coin is dropped Sibille's right hand covers last fortune shown. Bowing slowly she raises her hand to allow a new "hand" of playing cards to appear. Simultaneously a card bearing a printed reproduction of this "hand" and also a clever reproduction of the fortune is thrown into the cup in front of machine. Additional cards can be obtained at small cost. 1,200 cards are furnished with each machine.

The outer case of the Sibille is remarkably handsome, made of highly polished mahogany with beautifully decorated glass signs, nickeled ornaments and handles with handsome antique shield.

The mechanism is strong and not liable to get out of order. Money box is separate and has an individual key. Made for nickels or pennies. In ordering state which is desired.

Height 94 in. | Depth 28 in.
Width 36 in. | Ship. Wgt. 565 lbs.

SIZE
Height 93 in.
Width 30 in.
Depth 11 in.
Ship. Wgt. 200 lbs.

Arcade Machines: 1912 Catalogue: Mills Novelty Company, Chicago

Automatic Bowling Alley

A Glance Shows this to be a Money Getter

A Ten Pin Alley complete in every detail which can be used with splendid results in Amusement Parks or placed on percentage in various locations and *cigars given as rewards for good bowling.*

The operation consists in placing a coin in the slot and pressing down on the crank at the side. This causes a ball to shoot out of the *aiming tube* in front. This tube is movable and the skill used in aiming to knock down the pins makes the game *exceedingly fascinating and popular.* Pressing on the knob at the top causes the pins that have been knocked down to return to an upright position ready for the next shot.

Finish: Polished Oak Cabinet with Nickel Trimmings.
Dimensions: Width, 10 in. Depth, 22 in. Height, 64 in. Weight, 75 lbs. each. Boxed, 110 lbs.

Automatic Bowling Alley

═══ Counter Style ═══

The Greatest Little Money Getter Ever Produced

Here is a little Counter Ten Pin Alley complete in every detail, just the machine to place on a Shelf Bar or Counter where floor space is limited.

The little Ten Pin Alley will attract attention wherever placed as everybody likes to try his skill in knocking down the pins which makes the game *exceedingly fascinating and popular* and at the same time the machine is gathering in the pennies.

In operating this machine it is a mighty good plan to offer rewards in *Cigars or trade for good bowling,* this will increase the earnings 500 per cent. and still the machine is absolutely legitimate in every way.

Finish: Highly Polished Oak Cabinet with Nickel Trimmings.
Dimensions: Length, 26 in. Width, 10 in. Weight, boxed, 40 lbs.

Automatic Pulling Machine

Cabinet Style — The Most Unique Pulling Test Ever Produced

Designed Specially for Amusement Parks and Pleasure Resorts

Its strange, unique appearance makes it a great drawing card.

Dial registers to 1,000 pounds. Electric bell rings at 750 pounds and a "devil's" head appears at the top.

In pulling the rope one or two hands may be used.

The Tug of War is a good "puller" and there is a place in every public location for one of these machines.

Handsome hand-painted sign surmounts cabinet.

Finish: Handsome Quartered Oak Cabinet, finely finished—the figure in a special process enamel.

Dimensions: Width, 20 in. Depth, 14 in. Height, 84 in. Weight, 190 lbs. Boxed, 260 lbs.

Automatic Pulling Machine

Platform Style — Can You Raise The Devil — A Pull of 750 Pounds Will Do It

Exactly the same construction as the Cabinet Mickey Finn except without Cabinet.

A Strong "Puller" in any location.

Dial registers to 1,000 pounds and Electric Bell rings at 750 pounds In pulling the rope one or both hands may be used.

Handsomely finished in brilliant enamels.

Large hand-painted sign in a strong well made frame.

The figure is of iron and very strongly assembled. It is mounted on a reinforced platform of oak with a rubber mat.

Dimensions: Width, 18 in. Depth, 10 in. Height, 72 in. Weight, 140 lbs. Boxed, 210 lbs.

Arcade Machines: 1913 Catalogue: Caille Brothers Company, Detroit

Rubber-Neck Blowing Machine

A Novel Lung Test, Large and Attractive

Every man likes to know that his lungs are sound and powerful — hence this machine is very popular and a quick money-getter.

Attracts all Classes

When a coin is deposited in the slot a steady blow on the mouthpiece, which is attached to a rubber tube, slowly **raises the Coon's Head** from the shoulders and he "rubbers" around as it raises. His typical long "rubber neck" attracts the attention of all, evoking laughter and mirth. A dial indicates the strength of the lungs. At 250, six colored electric lights show; and at 500, a large electric bell rings.

Special Feature: If 500 is registered money is returned into cup in front automatically.

Finish: Designed especially for Amusement Parks and Pleasure Resorts.

Elaborate polished oak cabinet. French plate glass, nickel or antique copper trimmings, separate money compartment under Yale lock.

Dimensions: Width, 28 in. Depth, 20 in. Height, 94 in. Weight, 200 lbs. Boxed, 270 lbs.

Before concluding, however, I want to give you a review of the chief points which should be considered in the establishing of an Arcade enterprise.

The first is location. There are two kinds of locations which are desirable for Arcades. One is the prominent retail street where the better class of people pass constantly, and the other is where the working classes gather in the evenings, but this point must be borne in mind: that the location must be a busy thoroughfare and it is further advisable to choose the part of the street where people are accustomed to congregate in the evenings and on Saturdays. It is better to pay a large rental and get the right kind of location.

The second point is that concerning the kind of machines. Experience has taught all of the big Arcade people that it does not pay to buy cheaply made, poorly constructed or secondhand machines.

The third point to consider is the decoration of the establishment, and this is one which is very important. The ceiling should be well filled with frosted globes, so that the light will not be too glaring to hurt people's eyes, thereby making it difficult for them to see the pictures in the machines, but bright enough to make the place attractive, with signs giving notice to the public that their wants are being carefully looked after.

Fourth and last, the enterprise should be handled as a business proposition from the start. It almost goes without saying that it should be kept scrupulously clean at all times. There should be no disorder and there should be no improper characters permitted. The very best elements should be catered to and made to feel that their wants and wishes are being respected. An occasional word or two in the local column of the newspapers about new songs, or some new, novel and interesting views just received will help wonderfully to stimulate interest and it is possible for an enterprising manager to get up teams to play matches in your parlour with the various athletic machines, lung testers, etc.

This is a healthy amusement for all parties concerned and should be distinctly popular with young men's clubs and organisations of a similar character. The plan adopted by many Arcades for attracting people from the street is to have some good musical instrument near the front of your Arcade which will play popular airs at close intervals through the day . . .

In conclusion, I want to say that if you are uncertain as to whether or not you are in a position to engage in this enterprise and will write to me telling just exactly what your circumstances are, I will try to show you some means of embarking on this splendid business. I put in 141 arcades last year and many of them are making more than 100 per cent. I am going to install five hundred this year (1907) through the West and Middle West. My factory is in readyness, the raw material is ordered, the locations are waiting. Your word only is needed to set the wheels in motion. Speak it!'

THE : OWL.

An Automatic Five=Slot Machine.

Purely Mechanical.—No Electricity.

IT WORKS BY GRAVITY ALONE.
Gravity is always active.
Always in working order.

***

Pays all Prizes in Nickels.

***

Coin Detector.

Always Shows Last Three
Nickels Played on Each
Color. . . . .

***

Can't Become Clogged.

***

You just push slide-bar and
pull the handle to operate it, then
let go; don't have to hold it down.
Five can play as well as one.

Draws Business
and
Does Business.

STRONG, SIMPLE, DURABLE AND ORNAMENTAL.

The Best Five=way Machine on Earth.

TESTED BY TIME!

WRITE FOR SPECIAL PRICES AND FURTHER PARTICULARS.

1898 Advertisement for Mill's Owl

CHAPTER THREE

Gambling Machines

We have so far paid scant attention to yet another class of coin operated machine, the gambling game. It was to be this class of machine more than any other that was to ensure that coin freed devices reached literally into every nook and cranny of society. Of all coin operated machines the gambling game was to be the most versatile since it could be operated in almost any location. Unlike the vending machine it was safer to operate in that it never offered the player a tangible commodity other than the money previously inserted by other players. Theft from such a machine was not theft directly out of the operator's pocket. The promise of easy money ensured (for a well designed machine) an enormous amount of repeat play, making it all in all, a low investment, high earning proposition.

Although the first purpose made coin operated gaming machine dates back to 1876 (following the introduction on a small scale of a countertop game in New York, by Edward McLoughlin, known as the Guessing Bank — the player had to guess the number the pointer would stop at before inserting his coin), the automatic gambling game was essentially a by-product of the automatic revolution of the late 1880s. Indeed, gambling by machine or otherwise, was furthest from the minds of the majority of our early revolutionaries. Yet once such devices had been placed on the market the extremely high income they generated could not be ignored.

Gambling Laws

Unlike most other forms of automatic machine, the existing gambling laws in Western Europe and North America were to lead to a divergence in the development of the coin freed gambling game. In Britain the 1853 and 1854 Betting and Gaming Acts were in force, setting severe restrictions on all automatic games of chance years before their actual invention. As far as the law was concerned the fact that a gambling game was coin operated made not one scrap of difference. The same was to apply by and large to other European countries, in France for example, an edict of Louis XVI issued in 1781 was still in force which prohibited all gaming for money. It was to have more or less the same effect. The gaming laws of the United States, where they existed, tended on the whole to be more liberal. It is primarily for this reason therefore that the automatic gambling game was to develop and flourish to a far greater extent in North America in the following decades, and not as our American contemporaries would have us believe because of 'backwardness' on the part of our European forebears. Indeed, in some respects, the reverse was to be true, since most of the major innovations in early gambling game design in the United States were implemented by newly arrived European immigrants.

The prime outlets for such devices were to be public houses and saloons, although they were to be found in almost any location possible, from the grandest restaurant or hotel, to the humblest corner shop. Public houses and saloons in particular during this period, must in many instances have rivalled the automatic shops or arcades, where gambling games were to be found in great numbers.

Initially there were to be few legal difficulties because the authorities tended to regard such devices as insignificant trivia, although the rapid rise in popularity of such machines during the 1890s inevitably brought them into conflict with the authorities, who by the turn of the century had begun an active and systematic campaign against such machines on the grounds that they led to the corruption of society. The end result of this was that European manufacturers on the whole had to concentrate their efforts upon the production of relatively low payout 'skill' machines. (Under British Law for example, the legitimacy of a gambling game was determined by the degree of skill required to play it since games of skill per se were legitimate).

Manufacturers and operators were therefore obliged to walk a tightrope of contention. On the one hand such devices had to have enough of a chance element to ensure that a skillful player could not win repeatedly, while on the other hand allowing for sufficient skill to satisfy the authorities. The solution adopted derived ultimately from the traditional fairground 'drop case' games, whereby a marble or ball was dropped through a series of pins into numbered compartments. As easy as the process looked it was difficult enough to ensure against a player being consistently successful whilst at the same time (in later variations of the game) it ensured some measure of protection in that success on the machine could be deemed a skilful act. Consequently, this format and its derivatives were to become the most successful type of gambling game in Britain until the coming of the three reeler in the early 1920s.

French manufacturers were also to be faced with similar problems, and were by and large to adopt similar solutions. The one major difference was to be their use of spinning dial games. These were permissible because under French law games of chance were not illegal, they only became illegal if played for monetary gain. After some confusion and much harassment by the authorities the law was to be clarified in 1909 by the passing of a decree which permitted games of chance but only so long as they paid out a maximum in trade tokens worth no more than three times the original stake (commonly 10 centimes). As a consequence of this concession spinning dial games were to prove particularly popular in France, and were to be manufactured in quantity by indigenous companies up until the middle 1930s.

Erroneous claims have been made in the past concerning the antiquity of many of the French automatic payout gambling games. The overwhelming majority of them were to be produced in the first three decades of the present century and not, as is more fancifully supposed, in the last two decades of the 19th century. The development of these games, particularly of the spinning dial (or roulette machines as they were known in France) must therefore be seen within the context of the highly influential American gambling game industry at the turn of the century.

In America the legal climate was initially far more favourable than the European one, thereby enabling gambling games of all types to flourish. Although drop case games enjoyed an early vogue, they were soon to be surpassed in popularity by the more lucrative spinning dial and five reel card machines. The dial machines in particular underwent a rapid development in the 1890s.

It must come as a surprise to many to learn that many of these early devices were designed to operate **electrically**. However, it was ultimately the mechanical versions which were most popular, so that by the turn of the century they were being made in large deluxe free standing cabinets, capable in some instances of paying out as much as forty dollars in cash — an enormous amount of money for that time. There was little impetus during the last two decades of the 19th century to produce gambling games whose principles of play were entirely new. The main aim was to produce a machine which was fundamentally an automatic adaptation of an already existing game. It is within this context therefore that one must see all the early automatic gambling games.

The relatively great legal freedoms enjoyed by American operators during this period enabled the American gambling game manufacturers to firmly establish themselves in the early years of the 20th century as a viable and rapidly expanding industry. It is therefore to this relatively early period that one must look to find the real reason for the later American domination of the world market.

The First Gambling Games

The late 1880s were to be key years in gambling game history, for in these years we encounter a number of very early versions of machines which were soon to become enormously popular. The earliest patent for a game of chance (McLoughlin aside) was granted in England to William Oliver in 1887 for a coin freed horse racing game which mimicked the large Jeu de Course gambling games commonly encountered in the casinos of the 19th century. These consisted in essence of a series of concentric wheels upon which were fixed toy horses. A player would bet upon whichever horse he thought would be the most likely to come to rest nearest the winning post. Although Oliver's machine was a relatively simple affair (it had no provision for an automatic payout) it was to prove popular. The genre was to be taken up by other manufacturers of coin operated games during the course of the 1890s. This class of game, as with so many other forms of gambling game, was to come to fruition in the United States in the early years of the 20th century in the form of freestanding automatic cash payout horse racing or roulette games which offered the player a choice of bets at differing odds. The mechanical development of such machines was to be intimately linked to that of the more commonly encountered vertically spinning dial games.

In 1889 the British patent office was to grant a second patent for a coin freed game of chance to yet another important pioneer, Anthony Harris.

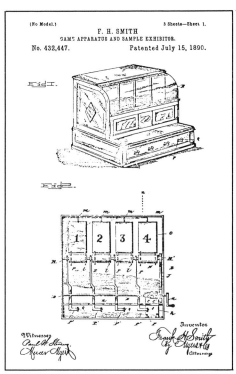

Patent: McLoughlin's Guessing Bank 1877

Patent: 'Game Apparatus' — Frank H. Smith, Ideal Toy Company, Chicago 1890

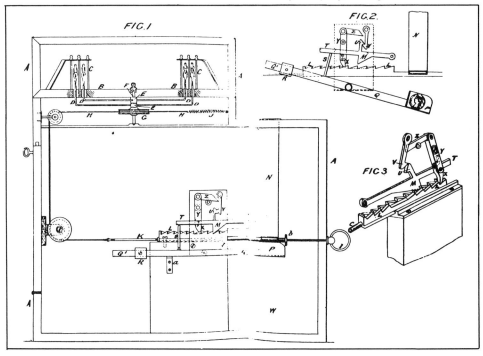

Patent: 'Improvements in Race Games' William S. Oliver, London, 1887.

This was for a wall mounted spinning dial game, and depending upon the dial chosen it could be used either as a gambling machine or as a fortune teller. Like the Guessing Bank it had no automatic payout and payment (if any) would be given by the operator when the dial stopped. With this machine in mind one must consider many of the early fortune telling games as potential gambling machines, since both were in essence games of chance and their function easily interchangeable. Indeed in later years when things were to get a little 'hotter' many gambling games were to be converted into fortune tellers!

Precisely when and where the first automatic payout gambling game was made, has not as yet been definitively ascertained. That machines of the late 1880s could pay out an article (primarily a cigar or cigarette) upon a player achieving a certain target on a dial (or even return a coin) by means of his strength or the electric current he received is amply borne out by a number of patents of this period.

This implies, therefore that had manufacturers so wished, they could have produced a payout machine, delivering at least a cigarette, if not a coin. Bearing this in mind, a claim has already been made for a spinning pointer machine made by an early French pioneer, Adrien Mays, known as the Musicienne. The year claimed is 1888, which is certainly possible, although there is no contemporary evidence to substantiate it. Its incorporation of a fully automatic payout would make the machine very advanced for it time, and in an industry prone to plagiarism the machine would have remained surprisingly uncopied for almost a decade!

However, to find the first substantiated claim for an automatic payout gambling game one has to cross the Atlantic to find the Eureka, made appropriately enough by the Eureka Box Company of Baltimore in Maryland in 1889. Essentially a drop case game, it featured a jackpot window full of coins. A coin inserted into the machine would occasionally fall into the jackpot. When enough coins had entered, their weight would cause it to tilt, making them fall into the payout chute. It was a simple device, hideously simple, the merest hint of violence would see it happily delivering the 'goods'. By the early 1890s the Eureka had been consigned to oblivion.

The year 1890 in America was to see the introduction of the Card Exhibiting Machine which, as its name suggests, was an attempt to mechanise a game of cards — specifically poker — a gambling game which had been very popular in the United States since the 1830s. The originator of this class of machine was to be Frank Smith of the Ideal Toy Company of Chicago who in April of that year was to patent the first coin freed card exhibiting machine. It comprised of five reels upon each of which was fixed a series of playing cards. The reels were spun following the insertion of a coin, in a bid to make up a winning 'hand' or combination of cards. Any award would be given manually by the operator either in cash or in goods. Over the next year or two a number of patents were to be taken out by other pioneers of the genre, most notably the firm of Sittman and Pitt of New York. Their improved Little Model Card Machine of 1893 had since been hailed as the first nationally popular coin freed gambling game in the United States, remaining in continuous production up until 1910. However, with the benefit of hindsight, it is a surprising fact that the vast majority of these early reel machines were to be manufactured and operated as trade stimulators which featured no automatic payout, with the spinning dial machines taking most of the technological limelight during the course of the 1890s.

1892 — New Developments

1892 was to be a key one for the development of the automatic payout gambling game on both sides of the Atlantic, for it is in that year that we first see the widespread introduction of such machines. In Syracuse, New York, the John Lighton Machine company introduced the Slot Machine. It was similar in principle to the Eureka: a coin inserted in the slot followed one of two courses — it either dropped straight into the cash box or it tripped a lever releasing two coins from the runway inside with the original coin plus the two additional coins dropping into the payout cup. More discriminating than the Eureka (it could take a little bit of abuse) it was to be an instant success and was to be copied widely in subsequent years.

That same year in England, Frank Urry patented and marketed the Tivoli. It too operated on the principle of the drop case game. A coin inserted into the slot would fall against a plunger. The player fired the coin by means of the plunger to the top of the pin bedecked playfield whereupon the coin would fall through the pins into one of a number of receptacles, falling either directly into the cash box or into one of four chutes which would return the coin to the player, or into the middle chute and thereby trip a lever to release a cigar delivery mechanism. The original cigar delivery mechanism was soon to be replaced by one which gave a card or a token. Although these were to be initially valued at one cigar they could in practice, as with the majority of all later token payout machines, be exchanged for cash. (Later machines of this type were to include tokens valued at up to 5/-, the equivalent of a 60-1 payout!). By the following year games similar to the Tivoli were appearing on the American as well as the European market. In particular it was to have a major impact on gambling game design in Europe, and was to be widely copied over the course of the next decade.

The year 1893 was to see yet another major development in automatic payout games. For this we have to return once again to the United States, to a small machine shop in San Francisco run by one of America's most important pioneers, Gustav F.W. Schultze. In August of that year Schultze was to be granted a patent for his Automatic Check Machine. It consisted of a dial divided into coloured segments contained within a wooden case. Insertion of a coin allowed a lever at the side to be pressed down, causing the dial to spin. If it stopped on a winning colour, a lever would engage in a notch on a star wheel inside the machine, a bell would ring, and two coins would automatically be released. A stop on a deeper notch would release a randomly packed token valued between twenty-five cents and two dollars. The coins or tokens were stored in runways (or chutes) end on.

Although practicable it was a relatively inefficient system since less coins could be contained within the machine, and variations in the thickness of the coins used often caused them to jam in the runway, one coin overlapping the other. The rudimentary system adopted by Urry a year

40

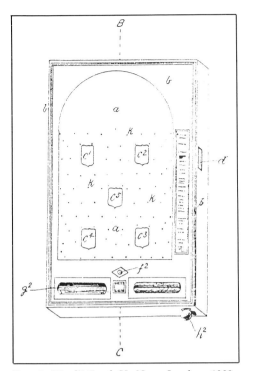

Patent: 'Tivoli' Frank H. Urry, London, 1892.

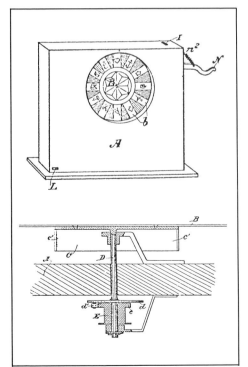

*Patent Drawing for 'Coin Controlled Apparatus'
Gustav F. W. Schultze, Berkeley, California, 1893.*

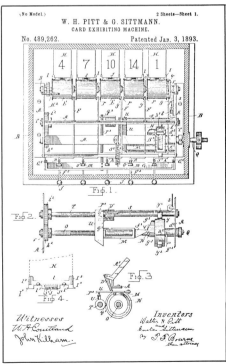

*Patent Drawing for 'Card Exhibiting Machine'
Walter H. Pitt & Gustav Sittman, New York,
1893.*

earlier in England was to prove more efficient, with the articles, cards, or tokens, being piled horizontally, and cut out one by one as the payout button was pressed. (Indeed, use of this type of delivery system in vending machines dates back to the early 1880s). In spite of this, the runway system was to be adopted as standard on subsequent payout dial machines in the United States until 1897 when the Mills Novelty Company of Chicago introduced the Owl, a large free standing dial machine that was to prove enormously popular. This adopted a more refined version of the tube payout system which automatically sliced out the coins from the tube in which they were contained. So popular was it, that by 1900 with the marketing by Mills of the 20th Century dial machine, the mechanism was capable of a top payout of 100 coins, each coin individually sliced out one at a time.

The United States and Europe Diverge
It is essentially at this point in time that the history of the payout coin machine in the United States and Europe diverges dramatically. In September 1899, the American Machinist wrote:

> That class of machinery in which you deposit a coin and obtain in return your correct weight, a sight of some model working, hear a popular air, get a stamped envelope, your photograph, liquid refreshment, kinescopic sights and photographic results, etc. etc., has had a remarkable growth. In the earlier period of its history the purpose of the makers was blameless enough, but in these latter days the machines have been adapted to cater for the wants of those who enjoy the 'taking of chances.' Accordingly, a numerous family of this type of machine has come into being, and has flourished and fattened on the public purse, or at least, the funds of that section of the public which needs considerable legal intervention and guidance to protect it from itself.'

Though these sentiments were to be expressed many times in America in the ensuing decades, it was to be many years before the country was to see any systematic moves to ban or control such machines. Their enormous success was to literally fill to overflowing the coffers of many of the leading manufacturers. The Mills Novelty Company for instance (effectively founded in 1897) sold something like 10,000 Owl or Owl related machines by 1900, at a cost ranging down from $150-$75 per machine, thereby granting them the financial viability necessary upon which to found their future manufacturing empire. This was only possible however, in so far as the authorities permitted the use of such devices. Since each area of the United States was governed by what were essentially a different set of laws, the prohibition of such devices in one particular area did not necessarily affect the overall size of the market. Indeed the early fortunes of one particular company, that of O. D. Jennings, founded in 1906, were based upon exploiting such a system. Jennings would buy the machines of operators in newly closed areas at distress prices, and sell them at a premium in areas unaffected by such laws.

42

AUTOMATIC MACHINES.

This is an age of machinery, automatic and otherwise, and to attempt to put a cog in its wheels would be just as effective as Mrs. Partington's broom or King Canute's command to stop the motion of the sea. Time was when these machines were confined to those which supplied you with a pennyworth of sweets for your money. You always paid, but you did not always get the

The "Tivoli" Machine.

sweets. There certainly was much more chance than skill in that kind of game, and the machines, like the banker at Monte Carlo, often got the best of the bargain. Of late years a vast amount of progress has been made in the construction of automatic machines, and one can now get a large variety of things out of them, from oranges to hot tea or coffee. We fancy, too, that they are more honest than they were of yore. The Automatic Machine Company, Ltd., have from time to time

The "Barrel" Machine.

placed a large number of most ingenious contrivances on the market for setting up in public-houses and other places of resort. Without any trouble or expenditure an hotel-keeper is able to add £50 a year to his income. We had the pleasure of witnessing the performances of a number of them a few days ago, under the able supervision of one of the courteous and urbane managing directors. If all the patrons of the

machines were as adept as he is in working the machines, we fear the company would not make a very large dividend. The machine we saw first is called "The Tivoli," of which we give an illustration. It has half a dozen rows of headed pins stuck on its face. The centre avenue leads into

Palace Billiards.

a drawer which sends out a ticket which enables the player to obtain from the bar a 2d. cigar, whilst two other avenues return the penny back to the player. We did not try the machine ourselves, but we were informed that players soon get very expert, and learn exactly how much strength to put in the pull. Mr. Wood, in our presence, had four tries. Three times he got his penny back, and the other time he got a ticket for a 2d. cigar. He thus obtained 5d. for the 4d.

Fairplay Skill Teller.

expended. The "Barrel" machine (which we reproduce), though differently constructed, is on much the same principle. It takes its name from four small barrels, into one of which you have to try to send the penny. If you do you get the 2d. cigar ticket. If you send it in either of the other barrels, the penny comes into play again, but is lost if you shoot beyond the barrels. Another kind of machine is called "Palace Billiards." Here, after having placed the penny in the slot a ball is released, which, when you pull the spring, moves up a column, either into the bull's-eye, when you get the 2d.

Advertisement for machines manufactured by Haydon & Urry Ltd, London 1900.

Perfection Card Machine

for pennies or nickels.
Size 16x10½x8½ in.
Weight 10 lbs.

Price $7.50, Spot Cash.

The lowest priced reliable machine on the market.

All machines guaranteed in writing.

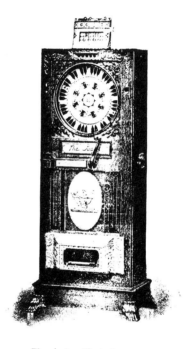

The Judge.

A 5 way winner. An attractive machine which will get the play. Has color register and coin detector.
Price reduced—write for it.

The Little Monte Carlo.

A roulette cigar machine for counter use. A trade stimulator.

Price $11.00 Spot Cash.

Free repairs furnished for six months.

The Judge Musical....5 way.

Is similar in every respect to the Judge regular, except that it has a high grade musical attachment, so connected that a play on the machine starts the music and changes the tune automatically, thus giving you a tune with each play. The musical attachment is contained in an ornamental case at the bottom of the Machine.
Write for our liberal offer covering this and other machines.

Advertisement for machines manufactured by Mills Novelty Company featured in Albert Pick & Company, Chicago, catalogue 1901.

The situation in European countries was to be markedly different, as any law applied to the country as a whole, and not just to any particular area, although in practice there could be slight variations.

Juvenile Deprvity
In Britain, with gambling games seemingly everywhere (in public houses, shops and arcades), the axe finally fell. What were once seen only ten years earlier by the authorities as mere trivia, suddenly began to be seen as a menace. Gambling games were everwhere, public morals had to be safe-guarded. The first three years of the 20th century were to witness a spate of prosecutions, particularly in London. In April 1902 a meeting was called by a number of prominent personalities in the industry, in which the following resolution was passed:

> The recent action of the Commissioner of Police, in initiating prose-cutions against the use of automatic machines, has caused 5,000 workmen to be thrown out of employment, whilst upholding the Commissioner's actions in the direction of suppressing juvenile depravity.

Juvenile depravity in 1902! Some things never change!

> With reference to halfpenny machines, it is considered unreasonable that after about 10 years usage of certain automatic machines on licensed premises without any complaint of gambling, that the 17th Section of the Licensing Act 1872 should be used as a lever for their abolition. Further, that as under the Child Messenger Acts, children under 14 are now practically excluded from public houses, the existence of automatic machines on licensed premises cannot be held as a means of juvenile depravity. It is decided that a committee be formed for the purpose of taking further action, especially in the direction of a deputation to the Home Secretary.

It was to be of little if any avail; the following year was to see a major test case, that of Fielding v Turner in which a sweetshop owner was charged and found guilty under section 4 of the Gaming House Act of 1854, for illegally using a game of chance. In order to avoid the further attentions of the police, payouts on machines in public places were henceforth kept deliberately low, in many instances offering the player no more than his money back if he won. (It is for this reason also, that it is virtually impossible to find a makers name or address on the vast bulk of automatic gambling machines produced, making today's job of identification that much more difficult.) The nature of such games had to change, if they paid out money or money's worth over and above the original stake the only defence that could feasibly be maintained in court was whether the game in question was one of skill or chance. It was because of this that the Pickwick patented by Henry Pessers in 1900 was to sweep the field over the next decade. It too was based upon the drop case games of earlier years, but with one crucial refinement: a ball was projected up to the top of the playfield by means of a plunger and after falling through a series of pins the player attempted to catch it by means of a moveable cup.

The application of the law over the next few years was patchy, in some areas even games that only returned the player's coin were prohibited (including some arcade shooting games). In other areas there could be a virtual free for all, in so long as it was discreet and sweet — sweet that is, in terms of the local constabularies pockets! Some areas were to witness some quite amazing scenes. In Sunderland, for example, in May 1912, 121 people were arrested, men, women and children — the entire clientele of an arcade — of whom 109 were to be charged on grounds of illegal gambling!

However, although prosecutions across the country were to continue, the year 1912 was to be a watershed year for the gambling machine. In that year, in a prosecution brought against it, Justice Scratton declared that the Pickwick was a legal game, in that it required skill to play it. There was an appeal against the decision in the following year, where once again the verdict was upheld — henceforth, any such machine worth its salt proudly bore a label proclaiming to all and sundry (particularly the boys in blue) the judge's favourable verdict! In spite of this, an acquittal could not be guaranteed. By 1914 in order to allay prosecutions electric shock attachments were being added to gambling games. The playing of the game was an incidental bonus, it was argued, because people actually used the machines for the regenerative effects of the electric shock. To prove this little old ladies were dutifully trundled into the courts to affirm that this was indeed the case.

World War Boom!
With the outbreak of the First World War business was booming and there were soldiers everywhere, just itching to spend their money. Witness the following advertisement which appeared in the World's Fair in 1915:

> Wanted at once Punchball, Haydon and Urry machines, Grip, Electric Grip, or any other machines to take money. Buy or Hire. There are plenty of soldiers here, and business is excellent. Shop in splendid position. Only 2 cinemas here. No other amusement. This shop will bear inspection. Call or write and don't delay as there is money going begging. Professor Leo Heath, Exhibition and Rifle Range, 79 East Street, Sittingbourne, Kent. I have a rifle range here. The talk of Sittingbourne which attracts crowds of soldiers daily.

Many new outright gambling games appeared in public, even the free standing pin wheel dial machines complete with high payouts and jackpots. It seems, from the nature of patent applications of the time, that attempts were made to modify them for use in Britain by the introduction of skill stops. Wherever success grew, the police were bound to follow, either to close the business or line their own pockets. 1915 was to witness a veritable flood of prosecutions but, unusally for the Press, the magazine John Bull was to spring to the operators' defence:

The spoil sports are renewing their pettyfogging activities in an attack on those penny-slot machines that are a welcome source of income to small shopkeepers and an incitement to adventure on platforms and other places where you wait. These enterprises in iron, commonly things of springs, balls and cups . . . are alleged to be affairs of gambling, or a lottery, or are stigmatised as wicked and shameful, and demoralising. Of course they are nothing of the kind. Nor are they illegal; even the Scottish Court of Appeal has given them a clean sheet as being games of skill and not of chance, and one can scarcely expect a better character for Godliness than that offered by 6 Scottish Law Lords. All the same there are prosecutions pending in the larger towns, notably Manchester and Liverpool, just because busybodies cannot keep quiet and must interfere. A smart defence in the case of a summons should secure its dismissal, for anybody who has risked a penny on one of these amusing machines must readily admit that success is not a lottery but one of cleverness and practice.

Automatic Defence Fund

Prosecutions however were to continue apace, so much so that by the following year in London an Automatic Defence Fund was established by operators to fight police harassment (the establishment of such groups is always a good indicator of hard times). It was to have little success, although the end result was to be the formation of the Amusement Caterers Mutual Benefit Society to act as a pressure group for the industry. By the end of the war things had started to quieten down. A 'gentleman's agreement' was struck in London, that gambling games could be tolerated so long as they only offered the original stake as the reward. With the war over, soldiers demobbed by the thousand; with the country in the throes of a depression and gambling games as a consequence taking less money, the legal climate gradually changed to one of toleration. Indeed by the early 1920s most court cases brought resulted in acquittals.

Can't We Have A Flutter?

Perhaps the best indicator of prevailing attitudes was the following report, featured in the World's Fair of April 1922:

> The Duke of York won a penny prize on Saturday, when following the example of his elder brother, the Prince of Wales he became a member of the British Legion . . . While at the bar he noticed a machine called the Invisible with a legend inviting visitors to try their skill. "Can't we have a flutter?" said Wing Commander Greig, and His Royal Highness promptly agreed. He ventured sundry pennies and after failures succeeded in winning a prize, a 1d check for which he received a box of matches in return.

Royal patronage indeed, but the future King's 'little flutter' was, as we shall soon see, to prove to be little more than the calm before the raging storm.

Liberty Bell: Chas Fey & Company, San Francisco 1905

CHAPTER FOUR

The One Arm Bandit

We must now turn to developments in America at the turn of the century where, as in Britain, coin operated gambling games were to be found everywhere. Unlike Britain though, the variety of such machines in public usage was greater. There were machines with one or more spinning dials or pointers, from small countertop affairs to large free standing cabinets. There were reel games, comprising of one, three, or more commonly five reels. Deluxe versions of the latter were also being made to cater for up to 5 players at once, comprising 5 sets of 5 reels — that's 25 reels spinning at the pull of one lever! There were dice games and drop case games in a wide variety of styles. Some of the machines paid out in hard currency, some in tokens, and some not at all. Some games in areas where the law was very tight were built on the 'runaway principle' (i.e. very small and light). Where the law was not so tight the machines gave out sticks of gum or played music each time the machine was used.

However, amongst all this plethora of devices, there was one machine missing — the automatic payout three reeler, now popularly known as the one arm bandit. Incredible as it may now seem, the first machine that everybody now thinks of when one mentions automatic gambling games, was to be a long time coming. Although claims for its invention have varied wildly over the years, placing it at any one of a number of points in time between 1886-1899 (thanks largely to latter day romancing on the part of its inventor) the first fully automatic payout three reel machine did not in fact appear until 1905 or 1906.

Charles Fey's Three Reeler

Its maker was Charles (or Karl as he would have been known back in his native Bavaria) Fey. It was without doubt a brilliant creation, one that has since milked millions upon millions of pounds out of people's pockets, but one which owes the greater part of its existence to the hundreds of people who came before Fey and pioneered the automatic concept. That is not to denigrate Fey, for he too was a pioneer in his own right. In 1893 he was to be found working as an electrician at the California Electrical Works in San Francisco. By the following year he had set up on his own account in partnership with one of the foremen, Theodore Holtz, as Holtz and Fey, suppliers of telegraph and electrical equipment.

By the following year both men had gone their own way, Holtz to establish T.F. Holtz and Company as manufacturers of coin operated machines (primarily card games), and Fey to work briefly with another pioneer Gustav Schultze. The following year was to see Fey striking out on his own as a coin machine manufacturer, initially of payout dial machines. From that point on Fey was to be his own man, making and operating machines of his own design. However, it was to be a localised operation, as none of his machines were to be produced in any great quantity or to be marketed on a national basis. In 1905 he engineered a variable automatic payout mechanism for a three reel gambling game.

Three reelers in themselves were nothing new, they had been around for at least eight years, and the fact that he adopted three reels as opposed to five was probably one of logistics, it being that much simpler to co-ordinate a payout mechanism for three reels. The principle used for the mechanical registration of a win had been established by his mentor Gustav Schultze in the early to middle 1890s on his payout dial machines. Similarly, his use of a variable automatic payout system based upon the use of payout slides was predated by the patents granted to the Paupa & Hochriem Company of Chicago in 1903 and 1904 for their Elk machine. Fey's genius therefore was not one of invention but rather innovation which made use of a number of previously existing elements in combination, to produce a new machine, the end product of which was the creation of one of the most tantalising of all gambling games.

The machine consisted of a rather drab cast iron cabinet resting upon claw feet. Insertion of a nickel enabled a player to pull down the handle at the side of the machine, thus setting the three, ten stop, symbol bedecked reels in motion — a perforated metal plate inside spinning with each reel. If a winning combination were made, the perforations in the plates would line up so as to allow metal fingers to project through them, thereby tripping a coin slide for a cash payout in nickels. In spite of the fact that the machine had an automatic payout, the award chart on the front listed drinks as prizes. It was a fairly standard ploy, adopted in order to deceive the authorities in areas where gambling was illegal into thinking that the machine was no more than a trade stimulator, in that it seemingly gave awards in merchandise rather than cash.

Another ploy Fey reputedly used was a tax stamp. Having used playing card suits as well as horseshoe, bell and star symbols on the reels, he stuck a two cent tax stamp on each machine — there being a Federal revenue tax on a pack of playing cards at the time. This in effect allowed the operator to further confuse the issue, by enabling him to argue that even if the authorities had refused to accept the machine as a trade stimulator, by the addition of the stamp it was in conformity with the law, being as much a game of chance as those played with a pack of cards. By this time artifices such as this had become increasingly common, and in retrospect it is evident that the automatic gambling machine has spent over half its production life posing as something else. Within this context even the name of the machine became significant. To this end Fey followed earlier precedents by giving his machine a patriotic name. He called it the Liberty Bell after one of the greatest symbols of American independence.

A Survivor of the 1906 Holocaust

In spite of a ready success, only a very few of these machines had actually been marketed by the time the city of San Francisco was to witness its greatest calamity. On April 18th, 1906 the city was struck by a massive earthquake, followed by raging fires. This event, as far as Fey was concerned, was to be recalled in somewhat romantic mood, many years later by his grandson Marshall A Fey:

> Within four blocks of Fey's shop five major uncontrollable fires broke out. Later in the day all hope of saving the area of the Market Street was abandoned. Charles Fey hastened to a nearby livery stable for his horse and buggy. Then he quickly returned to his doomed shop to salvage what he could. Fortunately he did save his most prized possession, the original Liberty Bell machine and a few lesser valuables.
>   After the fire Fey returned to find that the handsome edifice that housed his shop was in a complete state of ruin. The interior of the building had been completely gutted by fire. All that he was able to salvage was a mass of molten nickels in a cash can of a slot buried in a pile of rubble on the ground floor. He mounted the souvenir of melted nickels on a casting that he was to treasure for the rest of his life as a memento to the 1906 holocaust.

The destruction of the workshop, indeed the whole city, must have been a severe blow. Fey's version of events would have us believe that he just picked up the pieces and carried on where he left off until, in the following year, the Mills Novelty Company of Chicago who had a branch office in San Francisco at the time, were to steal one of his machines in order to make copies of it. True or not, the Mills version of events (as evidenced by Bert Mills in an interview given to Donald Barr of the Music Box Society in 1972) is more likely:

> The late Charlie Fey . . . came to Chicago with his hand built machine. He said to my brother that he would like to make a deal with him on this machine and acknowledge . . . that he could not protect himself since patents could not be secured on gambling devices. He offered to turn his design over to Mills Novelty if he could get for free the first fifty machines that were made. The deal was made on that basis. His machine was very, very crude. We went ahead and reengineered it and added a lot of parts. I did much of the development work and it was this machine that formed the basis . . . of many other machines produced by Mills Novelty.

Ring In the New
The Mills Liberty Bell was to be no mere copy of the Fey machine. It was more ornate and featured a bas relief casting of the Liberty Bell. It differed also in two more important respects. On Fey's machine only three symbols at a time could be seen in horizontal alignment. Mills increased the size of the window, thereby enabling the player to see the rows of symbols directly above and below the central win line, thus tantalising the player into prolonged play by showing him potential winning combinations.

Advertisement for Mills Liberty Bell, 1909 catalogue

Mill's second improvement was the introduction of the 20-stop 20-symbol reel system. Fey's original 10 stop, 10 symbol system allowed for a possible 1000 combinations (10x10x10). The Mills system (still in general use today) increased this to 8,000 (20x20x20), thereby allowing an enriched array of winning combinations, offering a higher potential return without affecting the machine's profits.

Within a few years other American manufacturers had followed suit; the machine as a consequence being effectively marketed on a national basis. Its advent was to sound the death knell of the older style pin wheel games becoming the major source of gambling game income, as witnessed by the following contemporary Mills advertising copy:

> Ring out the old, ring in the new machines and get a Liberty Bell. It is the most marvellous card machine ever manufactured. Hundreds of men have found the Liberty Bell a big money maker and you will find so too, if you give it a trial.

Symptomatic of the legal climate in various areas, the machine was marketed in a number of versions (operating on cash or tokens and paying out cash, tokens or nothing at all). In some areas, Louisianna for example, which in 1908 passed a law specifically prohibiting the use of slot machines as gambling games, the Liberty Bell was marketed as a vending machine.

The simple expedient that Mills used was to substitute the symbols on the reels — hitherto card related — with relatively innocuous ones bearing pictures of fruit. Why fruit? Because the machine was ostensibly nothing more than a means of advertising the different flavours of chewing gum available over the counter, a win on the machine entitling the player to the requisite number of 'free samples'. He could then go home and tell his friends just how wonderful Mills' new Bell Fruit Gum tasted! In order to emphasise the point, within a year, models were being marketed with gum vending attachments.

By 1913 yet another ploy had been incorporated — the future play. This was in fact a counter which registered whether or not a win had been achieved and the amount payable to the winner. The sting in its tail was that it delayed payout until another coin had been inserted, and the machine played. Manufacturers and operators could now claim that the machine was no longer a game of chance since the player knew in advance what he was going to receive. Even though the idea had not originated with them, the Mills Novelty Company even went to the extent of hiring a leading firm of attorneys to examine the use of such a device in respect of the then current gambling legislation. They were to sum up the position as follows:

> We have no hesitation therefore, in advising you that in view of the law and the facts submitted to us, your machine is a legitimate one and its use cannot be prevented by any unbiased authority.

That manufacturers increasingly saw fit to use such tactics was symptomatic of increasing legal difficulties. Post World War I society in America witnessed the ascendancy of a movement which was to culminate in the passing of the Volsted Prohibition Act of 1920 — its primary aim being to abolish the manufacture, sale and consumption of all intoxicating liquor. The effect of this was to prove more damaging than the wave of anti gambling laws which had swept the country as a consequence of the Temperance Movement's success, because it's immediate effect was the closing down of all saloons and bars etc. on a national scale — which by that time had become the largest collective outlet for the automatic gambling machine.

Export Or Go Under
As a result manufacturers were faced with little choice but to look for another market. Coin operated machines had been exported to Europe by a number of American firms since the early years of this century. The vast majority of these were arcade games, but by the end of the First World War the variety had increased to include a number of gambling games (even, in extremely limited numbers, Mills Liberty Bells). The Prohibition Act was to change all this. The previous, rather casual export drive began to increase in earnest. Manufacturers had to export or go under.

Britain was in many ways a natural market, sharing as it did a common language and cultural background. These factors, plus the relatively relaxed attitudes to gambling games adopted by British authorities (as we have already noted) in the early 1920s, were to ensure that the United Kingdom was to bear the full brunt of this campaign. Machines were shipped to Britain and sold at 'distress' prices, thereby providing dealers and operators

Operators Bell: Mills Novelty Company 1913

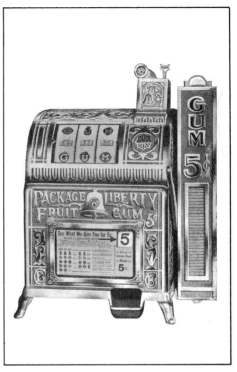

Future Play: Caille Brothers Company 1913

Sports Arcade, Brighton, c1926 (note prominent display of Mill's Front O.K. Mint Venders).

with enough incentive to buy in large quantities. An incidental benefit of this policy was that British or European manufacturers were from the outset unable to compete on economic grounds, thereby guaranteeing the Americans a virtual monopoly in the gambling game genre.

That British operators felt confident enough to place such an outright gambling game on the market at this time is attributable to a number of factors.

First, as we have seen, was the authorities relatively relaxed attitude to such games. 1923 was at least the third time in which the Clown, for example, one of the most successful of all wall machines, had been declared legal by a British court.

Second, the three reeler in its various disguises in the United States had had mixed results, not all negative. In Alberta, Canada, a three reel mint vender had on appeal been declared legal — a key decision in that decisions in British courts were held binding in Canada, so, it was hoped, the Canadian decision would have a reciprocal effect.

Third, the British automatics industry, after the heady days of World War I was (along with the rest of the economy) undergoing a slump, with few new devices being placed on the market. This ironically was to prove one of the main reasons for the three reeler's subsequent success, as evidenced in 1932 by the report of Eric King, chief of the specialities division of the US Department of Commerce, which stated "that during the hardest times in England receipts from coin machines actually increased".

By the time three reelers had entered upon the the U.K. scene they were

Gathering of prominent U.K. fruit machine operators c1930 to celebrate the arrival of Ralph Mills of Mills Novelty Company, Chicago. Can you spot the 'friendly' policeman? Here's a clue — look for the one with the bald head.

no longer disguised as gum venders (even though they still bore fruit symbols on the reels) but as mint venders. This had been brought about in the States following harassment by the American health authorities who objected to the stick gum that the machines originally sold, because of its short shelf life. The fact that it tasted terrible (the words 'powdered chalk' have been used in this context) was an added bonus. As a consequence, such machines by the early 1920s were vending rolls of mints, which might have resembled powdered chalk more closely but at least had a longer shelf life.

By the mid-1920s the three reeler was being operated in every part of the country, a fact attested to by the appearance and subsequent proliferation of advertisements relating solely to such machines in the World's Fair.

The machine's success during 1925-26 was little short of phenomenal with literally dozens of operating and distribution companies springing up almost overnight. By the late 1920s agencies had been established for the major U.S. manufacturing companies, not only to market their products in the U.K. but also in other European countries, primarily France and Germany.

In spite of the strictures of the law the machines were intitially tolerated, but when they began to appear in large numbers it became inevitable that action would be taken against them.

In 1926 the Chief Constable of Brighton banned their use, and in June of that year the first major case occurred. The defendant, a confectioner, was summonsed for using an illegal machine — a machine which in this instance had been adapted to give no mints, the player receiving a stick of Brighton rock over the counter to the 'value' of the disks he purchased.

The case was lost in spite of an appeal and much convoluted wrangling over the efficacy of the future play device. The court had accepted the argument of the prosecution that since a player could not affect the result in any way, it was a game of chance and it was therefore illegal. The fact that the player received a roll of mints, or in this case a stick of rock was deemed irrelevant as it was 'well known that most players kept putting money into the machines without even bothering to take more than a few of the packets, and continued to play the machine even if it was empty'. The British were evidently not a nation of chalk lovers.

Prosecutions
Prosecutions increased apace from this time onwards. In January 1927 the Daily Mail published a report in regard to pending court cases in London, writing of the determination of the authorities to put an end to these machines. This fanned fears among operators that there would indeed be a wholesale ban placed on them, whatever their shape or form and rumours even extended to the suggestion that because of this no more machines were being manufactured in the States.

However, the operation and sale of such devices had proved far too lucrative for them to be stopped so easily. The number of three reelers in London alone had conservatively risen from 140 in early 1926 to well over 8,000 by the end of the year. There was no other machine like it. It's use would not be given up without a fight.

The Fight For the Three Reeler — The Formation of B.A.M.O.S.

In December 1926 dealers and operators of the three reel machines in London united to form the British Amusement Machine Operators Society. Its purpose was a dual one. First, to counter legal action taken against such machines, and second, to harmonise relations not only between rival operators, but also between operators and the rest of the showman fraternity who resented the attentions once again being paid by the authorities to all coin operated gambling games. To many established operators this new 'diddler' breed (diddler was the term used in the 1920s to describe a three reeler) were little more than wide boys. This latter attitude was expressed in a World's Fair editorial which appeared in 1927:

> Anyone who is not suffering from the affliction that 'Fairplay' is a martyr too may ride on a bus through London or the provinces and see the empty shops labelled 'Fun Fair', 'Fair Ground', and 'Amusement Place' which were in most cases run by 'Mushroom' operators, styling themselves 'showmen' during the 'fruit machine boom' and it is these people who have brought the authorities down onto games which have for years been free from the official ban . . .

Relations between rival three reeler operators had also reached an all time low, the rush to cash in on the boom leading to cut-throat competition. Prior to the advent of the slot-machine the normal percentage of the take paid out to a location owner was 20-25%, but due to intense competition this had reached the ridiculous proportions of 75-80% making the letting out of machines 'more a labour of love than business'. This 'cutting' caused a great deal of friction between operators, who would often resort to other tactics. Employees would be sent round to 'foul' competitors machines (sometimes even competitors), the mildest form of which was the insertion of bent coins, in order to jam the mechanism. 'Topping' was also a common practice amongst the unprincipled, that is the siting of one's own machine in a rival's area. B.A.M.O.S. played a key role in harmonising relations between rival operators, and helped focus attention on the biggest threat of all, the Law.

A resolution was passed that a fund should be established to finance a test case in order to establish the legitimacy of the three-reeler in Britain. In order to have any hope of success, the machine used would be a mint vender complete with future play and skill control buttons. If need be the case would be taken to the House of Lords.

It was estimated that at least £4000 would be needed, and an appeal was made to the whole industry in April 1927 in order to raise the necessary funds. It was felt certain to succeed because:

> . . . machines were idle, operators and machines were doing nothing, shopkeepers were grumbling at the loss of customers and profit, and the public were resenting the taking away of machines from them. Showmen too were prominent in their complaints and would no doubt subscribe.

Views of Bolland's Amusement Machine Supply Company, London, Showrooms — early 1930's.

However, the appeal failed and less than £1000 was raised. Manufacturers in America (long since worldly wise) declined a contribution, saying that in their opinion the legal points of the three reeler had become 'somewhat obfuscated'.

In future years therefore, operators had to keep their heads low, or respect the time honoured tradition of keeping certain people 'happy'. Almost all of the successful operators of the late 1920s and 30s were to be regular contributors to some obscure branch of a police benevolent fund. This was successful in many cases and indeed one operator of note gave up his erstwhile occupation as Chief Constable in order to pursue a more lucrative career in the slot machine business!

The Formation of the A.C.A.

The friction resulting between the established showman fraternity and the new three reeler breed was to be highlighted in October 1927 with the formation of the Amusement Caterers Association which sought to promote the interests of showmen in general, who saw the three reeler as an unnecessary intruder, which would succeed not only in bringing the wrath of the authorities upon itself, but also upon all related games and machines.

The divide was further enhanced by their choice of parliamentary representative. Whereas B.A.M.O.S. had as their President Sir Walter De Freece, Conservative MP for Blackpool, the A.C.A. had Colonel Harry Day, Labour M.P. for Southwark Central — for many years a leading figure in the automatics industry. It was to be many years before the two rival associations were to unite to form one representative body for the whole industry.

In spite of the concerted efforts made by the authorities during the late 1920s to ban the use of such machines, the three reeler still had one last refuge, that bastion of British society, the private club. In 1930, on a number of occasions, their use in such a context was held to be legal. In that year Sir Robert Wallace K.C. ruled that their use in such a club or private house for the use of members was no offence against the law. This marked a turning point in the history of the three reeler, disappearing as it did from arcades, pubs and shops, and appearing mainly in the confines of private clubs, many of a somewhat bogus nature.

Since the early days the slot machine had undergone a parallel development in that the same model was commonly produced in a number of different versions, each made to suit the legal requirements of different locations. It was rare in Britain to see a machine in a public place that was not disguised in one way or another.

The strange legal position in Britain in 1930, although effectively banning its use in public places (at least not without disguise) now meant that in certain instances it could be used without any disguise at all. From this period, therefore, the importance of disguise lessens considerably.

A Royal Commission

In spite of this small measure of success the situation was not to last long. The law as it had been applied was essentially confused. Conflicting judgements had continuously been arrived at. Only in Scotland under the Gaming Act of 1917 was the law absolutely clear in its condemnation of these machines. In Britain, no case had ever reached the House of Lords, whose judgement would have been considered binding in all areas. Articles increasingly appeared in the national press urging that the machines be banned outright. The National Anti-Gambling League considered the matter so serious that they sent a deputation to the Home Secretary. In response to this concerted pressure a Royal Commission was set up in 1932 to 'enquire into the existing laws and the practice thereunder relating to lotteries, betting, gambling, and cognate matters, and to report what changes, if any, are desirable and practicable'.

In spite of the deputations made to the Commission by both B.A.M.O.S. and A.C.A., who judiciously avoided pressing the merits of the three reeler too forcefully, the Report of the Royal Commission in 1933 confirmed their worst fears. It stated that the gaming machines were undesirable; that the existing laws in Britain were fairly effective but should be strengthened.

No special exemption was proposed from the general provisions of the law in regard to games at shows. Automatic machines and like contrivances for the playing of games for a prize in shops, fairgrounds and other places or resorts should be specifically prohibited.

The 1933 report was to set the tone in Britain for the next three decades. The prevailing mood of the middle to late thirties is perhaps best evoked by the following anonymous letter published by the World's Fair in 1972:

> In the good old days, before we used to install machines in a club we used to drive quickly round the area surrounding the club to see if any police were patrolling there, and only then did we whip into the club with a machine clasped tightly to our chests. I well remember going into a local club with two Mills Golden Bell fruits and did my usual tour around, and then halfway across the pavement I was horrified to see a bobby come from among the market stalls about 100 yards away from me. I dashed to the club steps at a gallop and my momentum carried me up five of the stone steps before I tripped and went full length still clasping my machine to my bosom. Machines were too valuable to drop with the risk of damage and my ribs were so badly bruised it was weeks before they stopped giving me pain. So what? Ribs heal in time, broken castings never. These machines cost us £27 brand new from the States and with an average site giving a gross of say £3 per week, our cash to buy new machines did not come easily, and as the games were illegal there was no such thing as hire purchase on gaming machines. We would get a tip off when a certain site was due for a raid, so we dashed along and put in old bangers sometimes with no guts inside, and took out our good fruits, and when the boys in blue took our old stuff away we whipped back in again with our good gear. Those were the days when the operators took their chances and licked their wounds

THE LITTLE MAN WITH TWO BIG WINNERS

MILLS

"Silent" Jackpot Bell

AND

Modern Baby Scale

Silent Features.

Starts and Stops Without Jar.

Equipped With Pneumatic Pump.

Clicks Eliminated From Reels.

Silent Upper Pay-out Levers.

Silent Payout Operation.

Scale.

Skyscraper Design.

Choice of Attractive Colours.

Entire Column is the Cash Box.

Small Compact Size.

Improved Accurate Mechanism.

Orders Strictly in Rotation.

FULL PARTICULARS FROM OUR AGENTS OR DIRECT FROM SOLE EUROPEAN AGENTS FOR MILLS NOVELTY CO., CHICAGO:

SAMSON NOVELTY Co. Ltd.,

ROBIN HOOD COURT, SHOE LANE, E.C.4.

Telegrams and Cable Address: Nosmasty, Fleet, London.
Telephones: Central 2601; Central 3789; City 5069.

NOW ON SHOW.

Printed and Published by the "World's Fair," Ltd., Times Buildings, Union Street, Oldham.

Samson Novelty Company, London. 1931 Advertisement.

61

Victory Bell: Caille Brothers Company, Detroit, 1920.

CHAPTER FIVE:

Illicit Activities

The social and historical context of the slot as a gambling machine has inevitably tended to place it beyond the pale of 'respectability' and has therefore determined its use as being undesirable and, for the greater part of its history, illegal. However, the suppression of an object which can be seen by many as being 'desirable' merely encourages organised crime to flourish upon the supplying of that commodity, the more 'desirable' it is the greater the success of the criminal element. There is no greater example of this than that provided by the American social scene of the 1920s and 30s.

The organised illegal use of the three reeler or gambling machine was essentially a by product of an even greater illegal industry brought into existence by the American state itself when on January 16, 1920 the Volstead Prohibition Acts came into effect, forbidding the manufacture, sale and consumption of alcholic drink. By attempting to wipe out the previously legitimate drinks industry it created a tremendous vacuum which in pre-prohibition days was worth about two billion dollars per annum.

In the specific instance of Chicago, home of the slot machine industry, there was to be an even greater twist. As early as 1910 gambling games had already come within the sphere of influence of organised crime. The controlled operation of such devices rapidly became entangled with the long standing and overtly corrupt practices of the city's politicians, of whom the most notable was Big Bill (the Builder) Thompson. In 1915 he was elected for his first term of office as Chicago's Mayor, his election marking the beginnings of the great criminal morass that was to engulf the city. He literally threw the city wide open, carefully cultivating associations with people in the drinks, vice, and gambling trades. He could boast of friendships which ranged from Big Jim Colosmo, head of the city's vice rackets, to Herbert Stephen Mills, president of the Mills Novelty Company. Eminently bribeable, Thompson's administration was to oversee the growth of organised crime in the city. In 1920, such rackets had a relatively modest annual turnover of some $100,000. By 1927, the business had thrived to such an extent (by now under the direct leadership of one Alphonse Capone) that it could boast an estimated annual revenue in the region of $105,000,000. A breakdown of this figure puts it into perspective: $60,000,000 from beer and other liquor; $25,000,000 from gambling establishments and dog tracks; $10,000,000 from other rackets. Although we do not know the figure derived from slot machines as such, the revenue from these machines must have undoubtedly represented only a small proportion of the total sum (bearing in mind other far more lucrative forms of gambling e.g. horse racing, dog tracks and casinos).

The gangsters of the prohibition era were first and foremost 'bootleggers' or drinks men. The three reeler entered their field of operation because it had long since become one of the customary trappings of a saloon or bar, in much the same way as the operating of jukes was to enter the criminal field in later years. Indeed, in a world of 'real men' such devices were considered as little more than ' womens games', something to keep the little lady quiet whilst they got on with the business in hand. Al Capone is often quoted as saying:

> All I ever did was to sell beer and whisky to our best people. All I ever did was to supply a demand that was pretty popular. Why, the guys that make my trade good are the ones that yell the loudest about me . . . The funny part of the whole thing is that a man in this line of business has so much company. I mean the customers. If people did not want beer and wouldn't drink it a fellow would be crazy for going around trying to sell it. I've seen gambling houses too, in my travels you understand, and I never saw anyone point a gun at a man and make him go in. I never heard of anyone being forced to go to a place to have some fun . . .

An ironic statement, loaded with truth.

In spite of the relatively small role that the three reeler played in relation to the growth of organised crime in America it became a prime target for the media. In November 1932 Fortune magazine published what was considered by many a definitive article on the subject entitled 'Plums, Cherries, and Murder'. It purported to be an expose of the profits made by racketeers from slot machines. The article gave figures of $20,000,000 as the turnover from such machines in 1931 in Greater New York alone, and a figure of $150,000,000 for the whole of the country. (Figures which on closer examination appear to be grossly exaggerated). An interesting insight into the composition of the article was provided at a later date by Bert Mills of the Mills Novelty Company in an interview:

> The reporter who wrote the article came to me to ask all about percentages on reel machines. I made up all of the percentages from the very beginning. They had a phoney story on the reels and asked me to help them correct it. I helped them out, but they didn't publish it the way I told it to them. It was erroneous. . you see, they twisted the story. They took stuff out of context, and said that we said it. Like most reporters, they wanted to build up the story, and so they changed it to suit themselves.

However, it would be equally misleading to present the role of the slot machine in relation to the growth of organised crime as a totally passive one. On a localised level, in the streets say of Chicago or New York it was most certainly not, but then both these cities were rife with political corruption years before the introduction of such machines. On a more sinister level one could ask, if the information were forthcoming, just how close was the friendship between Herbert Mills and Bill Thompson? Or find significance in the fact that the export drive in three reelers began in earnest in 1923, the very year that Thompson was defeated at the polls by William E. Dever (at that time a seemingly clean politician). Other instances are forthcoming, but to imply a deeper involvement on the part of the manufacturers as a whole, other than one of economic expediency would at best be tenuous with the present available information.

Undoubtedly it was the machine's tangibility and its easy access as a commodity which facilitated its use as a scapegoat for the wider evils of society, the end result of which was to make the slot machine a major symbol of the corruption endemic in the United States. The more nebulous yet far more lucrative parts of the criminal empire which flourished around the prohibition era were far harder to assimilate as ready made symbols of corruption in the popular consciousness. With the imminent repeal of the Prohibition Laws in the early 1930s, due wholly to the catastrophic nature of their effect, it was inevitable that the actual, and more significantly the relative importance of the three reeler to organised crime would increase. The early 1930s were therefore presented as peak years of criminal activity concerning its use, as people were seen to be 'fighting for their control pending the repeal of prohibition.

The Pintable
As a consequence of these developments the United States (and similarly Britain and other European countries) was to witness yet another wave of anti-gambling fervour. It is within this context therefore that one must see the advent of yet another type of coin operated machine — the pintable. Although such devices had been around since the earliest days of the automatics industry, they had been, by and large, ignored. Essentially coin operated adaptations of traditional games, they had been regarded as a mere incidental adjunct to the automatics genre, in that they took a relatively long time to play (meaning a lower rate of return for the operator) and paid out no money (meaning reduced player incentive). However, the prevailing legal and economic climate of the early 30s proved, quite surprisingly, the ideal one in which such games were able to flourish to a hitherto unprecedented extent. The models in use at the end of the 20s (although many times since heralded as the first pintables) were in fact little more than latter day variations of an ongoing genre.

That they were to succeed in the early 1930s on a scale little short of phenomenal can be attributed to a number of factors. The three reeler and its attendant publicity had wetted the public's appetite for all coin operated games. More importantly the success of the slot machine in the late 1920s had resulted in a wholesale explosion of the manufacturing, marketing and operating industries. The legal difficulties encountered on an international scale ensured that this newly engorged market was left with a gaping hole; something had to fill the vacuum. Ironically as it turned out, the pintable proved to be just the thing. It had been around for years. In its earliest form, it was cheap to make and buy, meaning that anybody with a modicum of capital could enter the field (unemployment during this period was very high). It was innocuous. It had no automatic payout. It could readily be

CHICAGO AUTOMATIC SUPPLY COMPANY
EXPORTING AND OVERSEAS SALES DIVISION
11–15 ST. GEORGE'S ROAD, LONDON S.E.1., ENGLAND

SELECTION 'A'—PAYOUT
Choice of any models illustrated.

50. MILLS Q.T.

51. MILLS GOLDEN BELL

52. CENTURY VENDOR

53. WATLING ROL-A-TOP

54. MILLS SILENT

55. PACE COMET

56. MILLS RESERVE

57. MILLS FUTURITY

58. MILLS BONUS

Please specify coin play in English 1d., 3d., 6d., 1/-, 2/- ; U.S.A. 5 cent, U.S.A. 25 cent, or your own foreign coin.
All payout slot machines are available with Fruit or Number Reels as required.

Please keep carefully for your future reference. This is a selection of proven equipment. Any other information you may require will be airmailed promptly at your request. This sheet is one of a series issued as loose sheets to add to from time to time.

You can buy any type of coin machine from us.

We stock large quantities of Spare and Replacement Parts and Electrical Units.

1950's Advertising sheet issued by the Chicago Automatic Supply Company, London, featuring some classic fruit machines of the 1930's.

considered a game of skill, the object being to pot the balls into the highest numbered holes. It gave value for money — most early games gave the player 10 balls for his coin. That operators gave a prize for, say, the highest score of the week, could hardly be considered gambling.

The real take off point for such machines in America (and consequently Europe) came in 1931-2 following the introduction by two relatively new companies (D. Gottlieb and Co. and the Bally Manufacturing Company) of the Baffle Ball and the Bally Hoo. Both machines were to sell in enormous quantities in their first year of manufacture, 50,000 and 75,000 respectively. Within months, if not weeks, the world and his wife (including the major slot machine companies) were engaged in the production of these little wooden boxes. Much new blood was to enter the manufacturing and operating field, who owing allegiance only to such games, tended to fare much better and produce more successful models than the established slot machine companies.

The Pintable Craze

The years 1932-7 were the peak years of the pintable craze. Across the Western world pintable parlours sprang up almost overnight, featuring nothing but row upon row of these machines. The opening of Faber's Sportland, New York, in the summer of 1933 for example, was attended with much publicity. It featured eighty pintables in four rows and was to enjoy a huge success, with crowds at times up to five deep around each machine. Models proliferated and the original little boxes studded with pins very rapidly grew in size and became quite sophisticated pieces of equipment incorporating much electrical gadgetry and ingenuity.

Well aware of the public's over-riding greed, the underlying trend, particularly in the States, was to develop the pintable into an outright gambling game. Automatic payouts were introduced, the price of play was increased and the number of balls was reduced. This meant that in some instances the player's objective was reduced to firing one solitary ball at a cost of twenty-five cents up the playfield in a bid to land it in a hole that triggered a payout of $25. Indeed, had the pintable been allowed to develop along its natural course it would never have resulted in the game we know today. Many operators learned through bitter experience the consequences of such folly and were very wary of such new developments. Witness the comments of a World's Fair reporter in 1935:

> Manufacturers do not seem to recognise the danger of high coin chutes and payoffs, which will certainly kill the modern skill marble machine business and throw the whole industry back four or five years. Undoubtedly the city authorities will soon swing into action.

As a consequence many, particularly in Europe, were to shy away from operating the more blatant gambling game variations.

Looking for Sinister Undertones

The Press, as ever — on both sides of the Atlantic — maintained its attacks,

Little Duke: O. D. Jennings & Company, Chicago, 1932.

more often than not trying to find sinister undertones. Witness this 1935 'expose' from the Sunday People:

FORTUNES IN THE PIN-TABLE RACKET

75,000 machines have been shipped over from the United States in the last six months. Syndicates are all over Britain. One of the biggest money making rackets of 1935 is that of the pin-table saloon. Hundreds of thousands of these American made machines — so called games of skill — have been bought by huge syndicates throughout Britain, and some of the people are making fortunes out of the pennies of the poor, who imagine they can get something for nothing. Pin-tables have begun to pall in the United States, so the American showman has dumped his machines in this country. In the last 6 months alone it is estimated that over 75,000 have been sent across . . . (earning) . . . £50,000 per week. Big money is made in the provinces, operating from London, Manchester, Birmingham, Glasgow, Cardiff, and Leeds, these are all big centres for the syndicates. And the poor penny pusher has often less than a one in ten chance of winning.
In one part of the West End these arcades are bringing in over £50,000 per week in clear profit! . . . Youths and girls of 15 or less are employed in these arcades and corner shops throughout the country, and kept at their stands until midnight, and in some cases in London until long after that . . . being more than a little inquisitive, I tried to join the pin-table business, I spoke to the manager, they call him 'the boss'. But I found out that all the money was 'in the ring'. As a last resort I approached one of the many pin-table manufacturers. I wanted to buy 20 machines and set up in business; Yes simple, but why buy? I could have them installed and serviced free of charge. All I would have to do would be to pay the rental of a shop or small arcade, pay the assistants' wages, and income tax, and other overheads and draw 25% of the profit. They would have the other 75%, clear! I ASK YOU.'

Compare the preceding with a more down to earth approach to the business published by John Bull in 1937:

Pin-table Money — it amounts to £10,000,000 a year in pennies! . . . At first sight that figure of £10,000,000 looks very much like a fortune for a fortunate few, but on looking into it the reverse is the case; it means very hard work and often little profit. There are three sides to the business, and they are represented by the importer, the man who runs the machines, and the person who puts in the pennies; and the latter, strange as it may seem, is in as good a position as any.
   A penny gives you a good pennyworth of amusement, whether your score is good or bad, and if it happens to be good you may even win a threepenny packet of cigarettes.

Now you see it, now you don't, 'Hideaway' cabinets of the late 1930's. The machine showing on the left is a Mills Extraordinary, first manufactured in 1933.

In those two points lie two of the many snags with which the second person, the 'operator', has to contend. 'It's all very well for people to think there is a fortune in this business,' as one man, the owner of a medium sized saloon, remarked. 'Maybe you can show me where it is? See that fellow over there? Well, he has had forty packets of cigarettes since lunch, and he certainly hasn't spent 4s. getting them. The table he's playing on cost me £15. In a few weeks it will be like all the others — out of date.'

Many people call pin-tables a gamble. They are — from start to finish — and the players are often the smallest losers.

Three years ago, when the craze was still in its first wild stage, one man outlayed his entire capital of thirty odd pounds on three good second-hand machines. He placed these on a fifty- fifty basis, in three cafes. Today he owns sixty machines, and they earn him a net income of £20 per week. Good money, you say. It is indeed, but it is by no means easy money. We asked him how he earned it.

'From nine 'o clock in the morning until nine 'o clock at night,' he said, 'I am at the beck and call of any one of the sixty men who give my machines floor space. And that includes Sundays. I am on the very best of terms with all those people, because that's vitally important, but I cannot say 'All right, I'll be round in the morning.'

'The moment a machine goes wrong I've got to drive round and fix it. People tell me I'm a lucky man to have a car. Maybe I am, but I couldn't do without it, and let me tell you I very rarely get a chance to use it for pleasure.'

Such insights on the part of the Press were to be rare, as they concentrated in the main on the more sensationalist aspects of the automatics industry. The position of all automatic machines which gave out money or a prize over and above the player's original stake became more tenuous as the decade progressed. In Britain, surprisingly, one of the major contributing factors was to be the coronation of George VI — the very man who had had that little 'flutter' all those years before. 1936-37 saw a considerable increase in police activity against the illicit use of coin operated gambling machines, as part of a concerted drive to 'clean up' in time for the coronation. In January 1937, for example, following a series of police raids, there was a total of 27 club and 12 East End cafe proprietors appearing before the courts. Included amongst these were the proprietors of the Chelsea Club and the London Arts Club in Shaftesbury Avenue. In all cases the operators or location owners were fined and the machines destroyed.

A National Scandal
Events in Britain were reflected and influenced by events elsewhere, in both Europe and America. As in the case of Britain, large numbers of slot machines began to be imported into France in the early 1920s as mint venders. By the late 1920s such machines had been specifically prohibited by the French authorities. Up until 1935 coin machines of all types had had a difficult time in France because the Commison Des Jeux (a police

commission which was created to regulate gambling in casinos, clubs etc.) tended to favour the powerful casino interests, hampering the growth of the coin machine industry there. A ruling by the French Government in 1935 took this power out of the Commison's hands, declaring it to be incompetent, and gave it to the courts.

In 1936, against the international trend, more liberal laws were passed which resulted in a boom period for coin operated gambling games. However, for the operators, this happy state of affairs did not last long. In September 1937 a law was passed suppressing the operation of all machines in which there was an element of gambling, even if no cash prizes were involved. The cause of this was a national scandal which had resulted following an investigation of automatic machine activities in Paris and the rest of France, which had uncovered widespread attempts by racketeers to extort 'protection' money from any important operator of payout machines.

The Nazi Party

Events in Germany were to provide a somewhat bizarre contrast to those in other countries. As in Britain and France, three reelers began to be exported in quantity to Germany in the early 1920s. The operation of such machines tended to be allowed so long as the payout was in tokens to be used for re-play, or if they vended sweets. However, in January 1933 the Nazis came to power. In the following year a law was passed which permitted gambling for money. In 1935 the law was reversed. Gambling for money was now prohibited, but gambling for premiums in the shape of goods was allowed, but the conditions imposed made the operation of machines uneconomic. In practice double standards were applied. Machines which paid out in cash were allowed to operate quite freely in certain parts of Germany, in direct contravention of the law but with full knowledge of the authorities. There was one proviso, that a good part of the takings was paid over to the Nazi party. To ensure this was done operators were obliged to employ 'Brownshirts'or members of the party. It was, in the words of a contemporary operator, 'A political operation pure and simple'.

Chicago Goes Anti Slot Machines

In America, as we have seen, the role of organised crime had become a major public issue. The early 1930s literally spawned a new generation of anti- heroes for the media to publicise. Names like John Dillinger, 'Baby Face' Nelson, 'Pretty Boy' Floyd, 'Machine Gun' Kelly, Bonnie Parker and Clyde Barrow had become household names.

In the specific instance of Chicago the federal authorities had sent Elliot Ness and other government agents to clean it up. With hindsight their success was largely symbolic, yet it promoted a widespread public response against many of the trappings of criminal empire. The three reeler, amongst other coin operated machines, was the most obvious candidate. From the corrupt administration's viewpoint their suppression would placate the media, in that they would be seen to be combating crime, while at the same time doing little damage to their more lucrative criminal enterprises. In

Fiorello La Guardia having a smashing time in New York.

1935 the Chicago Anti-slot Ordinance was passed banning the operation in the city of all coin- operated machines. In 1938 the Automatic World wrote, with a certain degree of naivety, that:

> Chicago during many years has had such a bitter experience of racketeering, often at pistol point, that the authorities having lost faith in kid glove methods of 'cleaning up' decided that by a simple process of wiping out the whole flock they were destroying the black sheep among them . . . and the industry has taken no concerted action to counter this outlawry . . . it reminds us of the rhyme of 'Humpty Dumpty' brought right up to date:

> A Cheeky Coin Machine
> Sat on a wall
> That Cheeky Coin Machine
> Had a great fall
> All the machine makers
> And millions of Cash
> Couldn't do a thing
> To lessen the Crash.

Little Fiorello's Axe
A parallel situation to that experienced in Chicago had developed in New York. By the early 1930s under the 'open' policies of Mayor Jimmy Walker, gambling game operations had become centralised. By 1933, Walker, facing charges of political corruption had been forced to resign. He was replaced by Fiorello H. La Guardia who in response to media pressure embarked upon a widely publicised crusade against gambling games, vowing to run them out of the city. Newsreels of him, literally axing his way through machines were shown in cinemas across the country. Like a latter-day Carrie Nation, his was the most symbolic gesture in the anti slot movement which was to culminate in the Johnson Act of 1951 banning the sale, manufacture and operation of all gambling games. By 1938, 45 of the States had banned the use of virtually every type of payout game, setting the seal on a legal situation which is only just now changing in America.

Whilst such moves were to make things even more lucrative for the crooked operator (they always do), they were to adversely affect the major manufacturers by severely reducing the size of the overall market. Many of the bigger concerns in Chicago, as a means of maintaining profitability, were to turn to the production of other items (notably vending machines, furniture, and domestic electrical appliances) in addition to their regular products.

Paternalist Tendencies
It is important to keep the role of the gambling game in perspective. America is a very large country. By referring to the big time gangsters it might appear as if one were writing about the whole country. This is not so. Although there was organised crime on a large scale in a number of the major cities,

it succeeded nowhere to the same extent as in Chicago. If it had, then one would surely have seen a President Capone rather than a President Hoover or Roosevelt. The localised position throughout many parts of the U.S.A. bore a closer resemblance to Britain than to Chicago. However, the Capone era and its immediate successors became sheer spectacle on a Hollywood stage, blown up to the proportions of a myth as indestructible as Superman. The three reeler in particular became readily identifiable as a symbol of that larger myth and was condemned disproportionately as a consequence. The irony of the situation in Britain was commented on quite perceptively by the American journal Billboard in 1937:

> What a paternalistic attitude the British Government and upper classes assume towards the lower classes . . . horse and greyhound races have taken more than £180,000,000. The Betting Act legalises these sports. Ask any British distributer why Britain legalises racing and yet forbids the fruit or Bell machine, and he will reply: 'It is the old idea that the races are the sport of the upper classes, while fruits take the pennies of the poor, and the upper classes feel they must protect the lower classes against squandering their money.' The comedy of the situation arises from the fact that the lower classes are regular patrons of the races as well as the Lords and Ladies.

The history of automatic machines, especially the three reeler, is littered with contradiction, deception, and hypocrisy perpetrated not only by manfacturers, operators, and players on each other, but also at various times by the authorities. The German example instanced earlier, is the most blatant example of this. However, it is surprising how such a relatively insignificant commodity is capable of so forcefully demonstrating the latent perversity of society, particularly in respect to the attitudes of the so called 'ruling class' which internationally tended to be one of paternalistic platitudes regarding the saving of either the 'pennies of the poor' or their 'morals', whilst at the same time paying scant regard to the economic structure which is the fundamental cause of that 'poverty.'

In this respect the suppression of such a relatively insignificant item, although it can superficially be seen as a benevolent act towards people who can ill afford to lose their money, was in effect an unconscious political suppression of what has been termed by many as the 'poor man's club', by virtue of the fact that these same 'benevolent' gestures cease when they directly affect the vested interests of that class.

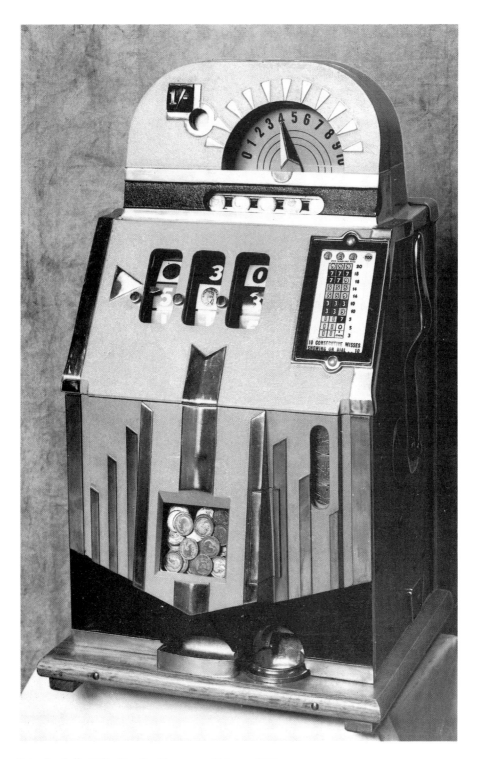

Futurity Bell: Mills Novelty Company, Chicago, 1937.

Model 200M: Automatic Musical Instruments Company, Michigan, 1958.

CHAPTER SIX:

Legitimisation

The tightening up on an international scale in the latter half of the 1930s had considerably reduced the overall profitability of many of the major manufacturing companies. The production of gambling games in America during this period underwent a triple, contradictory, and yet complementary development. Many more machines were made smaller and lighter than hitherto in order to facilitate the hard pressed operator, and resuscitate the 'runaway principle' of the early 1900s. Machines of normal size were also made, because they were ultimately more popular with the players. In the most difficult areas they were sometimes incorporated into 'vanishing' cabinets whereby the machine could be made to disappear into its own stand at will. Paradoxically, the greatest contradiction was provided by the introduction of The Console, which in fact represented a drastic increase in the size of the machine, thereby making it a permanent fixture.

The Console was an entirely new development of the slot machine, and was many years ahead of its time. In essence it was a free-standing, flat topped, electrically operated three reeler. Its development came about largely as a result of advances in pintable design, which by the late 1930s incorporated a large amount of electrical gadgetry. The market for this type of machine was however, limited. An operator could hardly be expected to tuck one under his arm each time the police made an appearance. In spite of this, its size did not mitigate against its use. Such machines were expensive to produce and were therefore designed primarily for use in private clubs, or in the illegal luxury casinos which were then flourishing in Illinois, New York, New Jersey and Florida, as well as for the increasingly important state of Nevada, which against all the trends had legalised all forms of gambling apart from lottery in 1931.

In spite of these 'guerilla' tactics on the part of the manufacturers, the overall size of the gambling game market declined considerably, and as noted in the previous chapter, in order to survive they had to diversify into unrelated fields. The entry of the United States into the war did nothing to ease their difficulties. As with other countries many companies closed down never to reopen. Those that remained were commandeered for war work so that for the next three or four years no new machines were produced.

The Mills Novelty Company
In the specific case of the Mills Novelty Company, diversification even forced a change of name. To maintain profitability they had engaged in producing amongst other things, soft drinks dispensing machines, refrigerator compressors, air conditioning equipment, ice cream freezers, and motion

picture projectors. Dealers in these lines requested that the name of the company be changed because its association with automatic gambling machines was detrimental. The change finally came following the awarding of a contract for the manufacture of bomb release mechanisms by the British Government who initially were reluctant to place any such order with a mere novelty company.

On September 1 1943, the Mills Novelty Company became Mills Industries Incorporated and a subsidiary company established, the Mills Bell-O-Matic Corporation, to market the company's post war line of slot machines. In spite of a short post-war boom in the automatic field things were to go very badly for the parent Mills company. Important deals relating to the manufacture of Coca Cola vending machines and juke boxes were badly mismanaged, resulting in a great financial loss.

By 1948, though still solvent, Mills Industries was experiencing great difficulties in meeting its obligations. It was put into a protracted state of receivership and in 1954 was finally liquidated. As its then President, Fred Mills Jnr. later explained: "We were forced into Chapter Eleven bankruptcy and lost the propriety to the products and the patents. We had to shrink everything down to liquidate. The guy who was brought in to do the job was ruthless, he just got rid of everything, the huge factory premises, all the fine equipment. The people who bought it stripped it down and made about $2,000,000. In 1941 the business had been valued at $10,000,000. It was a great shame, a great loss." The only section of the company that was saved was the Bell-O-Matic Corporation, which managed ultimately to prosper, even in the bleak years to come.

The Johnson Act
As this instance shows, the late 40s and early 50s were to be no golden age for manufacturers in the U.S.A. Anti-gambling fervour swept the nation once again, following investigations into racketeering, but in many ways fostered by the rise of McCarthyism; A Federal Bill was proposed which amongst other things sought to ban the interstate shipment of gambling games — a move disastrous in its implications to the manufacturing industry.

In response to this the industry united to form the American Coin Machine Manufacturers Association in December 1949, with Herb Jones of the Bally Manufacturing Company (one of the most successful of the pin table companies) as its president. Its aim was 'to work for the good of the entire industry.' The effort was futile, In January 1951 the Johnson Bill became law. It enacted that any violators of the law would face a $5,000 fine and two years' imprisonment. The law effectively made it illegal to manufacture, recondition, repair, sell, transport, possess, or use any gambling device in any land under the exclusive Federal jurisdiction. The manufacturers worst fears had come true. In February of that year Herb Jones was quoted by the trade journals as saying, rather lamely: 'So far as I know all manufacturers affected by the bill have already stopped making them. They stopped last week.' He added that some of the manufacturers were going into defence production for the Korean war. Just how harsh the implications of the bill were, may be instanced in the case of the non payout pintable, which was henceforth considered illegal in many areas even if it offered the player no more than a replay on the machine as a reward.

The law also enacted that any state wishing to exempt itself from the Federal Bill was able to do so, thus permitting the shipping of gaming devices into its area. This might have raised some hopes since two states, Nevada and Maryland, were to settle for this option. However, they were soon dashed, for the Chicago-based manufacturers, following the passing of a law by the Illinois State Legislature prohibiting all out of state shipments. As a token of defeat the short lived American Coin Machine Manufacturers' Association was dissolved to a backdrop of intense F.B.I. activity against unlawful interstate trafficking of machines. The Chicago based manufacturing companies that could not move had no option but to switch to new product lines or go out of business. The 1950s therefore were very lean years for the automatic gambling machine manufacturers, with few companies of any note left in the manufacturing field.

Nevada — An Oasis In The Desert
In 1931 the State Legislature of Nevada had passed a bill which legalised all forms of gambling, except lottery, within the state. It was passed at a time when the mineral mines, which were the main industry of the state, had become uneconomic due to the depression. The new law was seen as a way of attracting people and business to the state. In the eyes of the national press it was seen as an experiment that was doomed to fail. In the pre-war years the growth of Nevada as a gambling game centre remained retarded, but as the anti-gambling laws in the rest of America grew progressively stricter, culminating in the Johnson Act of 1951, Nevada and especially the towns of Reno and Las Vegas, became an increasingly attractive proposition for the diverse elements connected with the gambling industry. As a consequence its real development as a national gambling centre dates only from the immediate post war years. It was in Nevada therefore that the manufacture and use of the automatic gambling machine was largely maintained and increasingly flourished in the lean post war years.

The United Kingdom in the 1930s
The position regarding the use of the gambling game in Britain in the late 1930s was a difficult one. The decade had seen an ever increasing number of prosecutions. Three reelers in particular were presented by the media as being inviolably tainted with corruption and lawlessness. The fact that they were manufactured in America led them to be seen as if there were an Al Capone lurking inside each machine. The natural growth of amusement arcades at the start of the war was taken as evidence that the racketeering in America had spread to Britain. In February 1940 the Evening News published an article on the activities of gangs running protection rackets in London. It highlighted incidents of gangs fighting amongst themselves to 'protect' arcades from their rivals, the price of 'protection' being a percentage of the takings.

Electrically operated console: O. D. Jennings & Company, Chicago, c1940.

The position in Britain at the start of the war was in some respects worse than in America. With no new machines being made and with the older ones either wearing out or losing their appeal, operators had little choice but to look to themselves for a solution. As with America, manufacture of automatic machines had ceased. Companies either closed down or were commandeered for war work. An immediate solution lay in 'converting' old machines, in effect making them new models. The process had started as long ago as the early 1930s and was to reach its peak in the 1940s.

The immediate post war years in Britain, in stark contrast to the developments in the United States, led to a more mellow attitude on the part of the authorities in relation to gambling as a social activity. In April, 1949, a Royal Commission was appointed to 'inquire into existing laws and practices relating to lotteries, betting, and gaming.' It gave its report in 1951 reaching, what was at that time a radical conclusion:

> . . . that gambling is of little significance as a factor in the economic life of the country as a cause of crime, and its effects on social behaviour in so far as they were a suitable object for legislation were in the great majority of cases less important than was suggested by some witnesses during this inquiry.

The report made a wide number of liberal recommendations but fell just short of including the slot machine, stating that it should remain illegal

> . . . because it does not require the presence of attendants to give a prize, it is capable of a rapidity of turnover which would render that element of gambling no longer trivial.' In spite of this, the report was to remain a landmark signifying a substantial shift in government attitudes.

During the war, amusement arcades in Britain, as in America, had flourished. In 1941 a survey had estimated as many as 118 operating in London alone, although by the following year 49 of these had been forced to close because of bombing and wartime restrictions. In February 1947 the Coin Machine Journal summed up the position:

> Those sites that remained naturally reaped the benefit of the reduced competition. At the same time there were more people at work in this country than ever before, and the number was augmented by the large influx of service personnel from the allies. On the other hand owing to the necessary concentration of all our efforts on the production of war time materials most of the customary channels for spending were closed. As an avenue of escape from the rigours and hardships of war people were only too willing to avail themselves of all the facilities for relaxation and entertainment that were available, and in the circumstances it is not surprising that arcades proved to be a great attraction. On the whole therefore even more was got back on the roundabouts than was lost on the swings,

and contrary to what was expected, most of the operators who were still in business at the time found their takings reached a high level never known in the piping days of peace. This year however we have begun to descend back to earth, and many amusement caterers who lost their sense of proportion have suffered sad disillusionment.

Pennies From Heaven

Just how good the war years were to prove is instanced by the case of a London based manufacturer, Freddie Bolland, who having been forced to close down his manufacturing operation moved out to Aberystwyth and set up shop as an arcade proprietor. If what he had made before was a 'living' then this was heaven. The area teemed with soldiers on leave. They had plenty of money, but few places in which to spend it. The arcade operated from early morning until late at night, day in and day out, with people literally hammering on the doors as early as 6 a.m. clamouring to be let in. The constant pressure was too much for poor Freddie, who had hoped for little more than a dignified retirement, away from the bombing raids. He suffered a mental breakdown as a consequence. With the war over, and spirits revived, came the move back to London. The problem was, what to do with the money? He literally had tea chests of pennies all over the place. Not wanting to bank it, for obvious reasons, how could he send it down to London without the handlers knowing what they were carrying? An entire railway carriage was hired, and the tea chests, now

Las Vegas in the late 1950's: On view, Mills Bell-o-Matic 'High Tops'.

84

SCREEN STAR
1d. & 3d. Play.

MILLS GUARANTEED
JACKPOTS.
3d. or 6d. Play.

MILLS BROOKLANDS
TOTALISATOR.
1d.

Mills famous Bell Mechanism on all machines.   Prices as per Pamphlet.

Mid 1950's Advertisement for a range of fruit machine conversions produced by Tom Boland & Co., Leeds.

closed and carefully labelled 'machine parts' were dutifully loaded on and transported to London. Problem solved.

However, the disillusionment as instanced by the Coin Machine Journal, was to become all too real as the years progressed and the number of arcades decreased. In 1948 the number of arcades in London had fallen to fifty-three. By March 1950 there were only twenty-five left in operation. The reduction of the number of amusement arcades was a reflection of the malaise in the industry as a whole, the primary cause of which was the severe manufacturing restrictions in force during this period, coupled with a loss of consumer interest in products they had become all too familiar with.

The publication of the Royal Commission report came therefore at a time when the industry was undergoing a sharp decline. This was further evidenced by a Church report on gambling which stated that expenditure on all forms of gambling had dropped by about £50,000,000 in 1951. The total expenditure on all forms of gambling in that year was placed at £600,000,000. Of this figure only £8,000,000 was estimated as the total annual expenditure on 'other forms of gambling including fun fairs' in effect representing a decline of some £4,000,000 from the previous year. (The figures are also of significance in demonstrating what a relatively small percentage of the total gambling revenue that the automatic amusement industry actually represented).

The industry was consequently powerless to develop a strong manufacturing base at, what to many, must have seemed the most opportune moment for it. In retrospect 1952 was to prove a key year. In December of that year trade restrictions relating to coin operated machines in Britain were lifted.

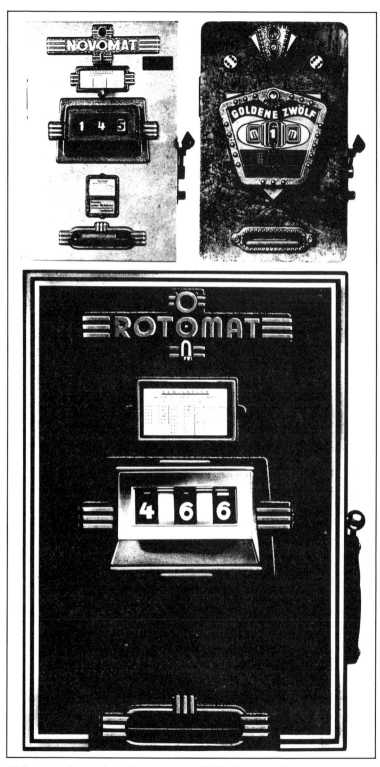

Wall mounted, 3 reel machines: Gunter Wulf, Berlin, 1953.

A year earlier operators and manufacturers in Western Germany had succeeded in getting the Nazi anti-gambling law of 1935 rescinded, and a new decree abolished the much disputed differences between games of skill and chance. Regulations were issued relating to the design and construction of automatic gambling machines which henceforth had to be licensed by the authorities. Towards the end of 1952, the German coin machine industry submitted a draft bill to the Bonn authorities relating to the use and manufacture of automatic machines. It was accepted and a new law passed on July 3rd, 1953. It was a significant development in that its successful implementation was to prove that it was possible for gaming machines to exist within a legitimate social context. More immediately it allowed the German manufacturing industry to take a much vaunted European lead in the production of machines. Immediately following the lifting of trade restrictions in Britain, German made machines began to be imported in ever increasing quantities.

The Juke Box
Before continuing with our narrative we must pause a while, to pay our respects to yet another phenomenon of the automatic genre, the juke box. As we have already seen with the pintable, the wholesale banning of what was perhaps the largest single sector of the automatic market (with the exception of vending machines per se), and certainly the most influential, was to leave a huge economic vacuum in the more legitimate areas of the market. Both gambling games and pintables had become victims of the anti gambling movement. Virtually the only machines which came through unscathed were those in the vending or service class, as long as they offered the player no premium.

For the many who sought to earn their living on the open market, this class of machine became the one safe bet. Amongst this class was to be found the automatic music machine which had been in use since the earliest days of the industry. It had not only taken money in its own right, but had also facilitated the use of gambling games in difficult areas. It was extremely versatile, and could be sited in a wide variety of locations. By the late 1930s, as the 'Juke Box' (its name deriving from the speakeasys or 'juke joints' of the Prohibition era) it had become a relatively sophisticated piece of equipment.

More importantly, it could be operated without legal restriction. Operators as a consequence turned to it in greater numbers than hitherto. Although not entirely free from allegations of corruption or subversion, the economic climate (initially in America and at a later period in Europe) ensured that from the 1930s onwards it was to have a virtually clear run. Legal moves in other areas of the automatics industry (which at times could verge on the ridiculous — witness the banning of plungers on pintables in one particular area) only made it that much easier for the juke box manufacturers and operators. If that wasn't enough, Hitler was to give them an even bigger present — World War II.

In-spite of the short term closure of most manufacturers of coin machines during the war, in the immediate post-war period the juke box

WURLITZER MODEL 2000
Offering 200 Selections

PLUS THESE TERRIFIC PLAY-STIMULATING FEATURES

GORGEOUS CABINET BEAUTY — 80 SELECTIONS IN VIEW AT ALL
TIMES — 40 TOP TUNES IN CENTER SECTION — 20 MORE ON
EACH PAGE OF MOTOR-OPERATED "BOOKS" THAT FLANK IT —
AMAZING HIGH FIDELITY TONE – SENSATIONAL CAROUSEL
RECORD CHANGER

The Greatest Entertainment Value Ever Incorporated in Any Phonograph

Distributor for Western Germany

GUSTAV HUSEMANN

IMPORT · AUTOMATEN-GROSSHANDLUNG · EXPORT
Komödienstraße 32 – 34 · Telefon 21 11 30 · 21 29 09

THE RUDOLPH WURLITZER COMPANY, NORTH TONAWANDA, N. Y.
Established 1856
EXPORT DEPARTMENT · ARTHUR C. RUTZEN, GENERAL EXPORT MANAGER

Model 2000: Rudolph Wurlitzer Company, New York. 1957

manufacturing industry flourished. The ensuing years of peace were to see the juke box thrive, as it had never done before, effectively entering its golden age, one which was to last until the mid 1960s. The puritanical post war climate also played its part in the irresistable rise of the juke box, in that it unwittingly fostered a youth subculture — essentially a revolt against these values, now known under the generic titles of Rock 'n Roll or the Beat Generation. By the mid 1950s there was to be something like ½ a million juke boxes in operation in the United States. By 1958 the figure had risen to ¾ of a million. It was indeed a golden age, when juke box operating figures were measured in terms of ratio of machines to population, and a popular story was doing the rounds, telling of a spaceman who had dropped in on Broadway from outer space. By chance, the first thing he saw was a shiny new juke box all lit up. At once the spaceman threw his arms around it and cried 'Gee! You're certainly the most beautiful girl on earth!'

The 1950s therefore were to be strange, if somewhat halcyon years for the coin machine industry. With the three reeler being forced to hide in darkened corners and gambling games in public use offering relatively modest rewards (witness the proliferation of sweet payouts in the U.K.), other areas of the coin op genre flourished; not only juke boxes (upwards of 63% of all coin machine operators in the States at that time considered themselves 'music men'), but a multitude of arcade related devices from shooting games to kiddie rides — themselves the subject of a mini boom in the mid 1950s. The public emphasis was set firmly upon 'family fun.' This trend was evidenced in Britain for example, by the sharp decline in the number of arcades based in urban areas, with a reciprocal increase in the number of those sited in seaside towns.

In spite of these developments, the three reeler was as ever to loom large in the public psyche. In September, 1952, the Baroness Ravensdale gave a widely reported speech to a rally of girls and mixed clubs in which she warned against the effects of TVs, cinemas, dance halls and slot machines, stating: "You are losing your hearts and souls in the torrent of all these inventions of the Devil!"

A year later the firm of Britvic launched a nationwide advertising campaign for their fruit juices, the centrepiece of which was of all things, a small plastic slot machine! These two instances, minor as they are, demonstrate the contradictory processes existing at that time, where on the one hand the paternalism of the system dictated that coin operated gambling machines be banned, while on the other, these very same machines having become such a part of public consciousness. Nowhere was this process more apparent, in the 50s, than in the United States. Inspite of a widespread ban on such machines in 1951, there was the meteoric rise of a city in the middle of nowhere (a desert is as nowhere as you can get) devoted whole heartedly to the exploitation of coin machines and seen by many as the natural place to take a vacation.

Reforms In The Law
The lifting of trade restrictions in the U.K. in December 1952 led inevitably

Sun Chief: O. D. Jennings & Co. First produced 1949. Versions of it were to be manufactured up until the late 1960's.

to an upsurge in the amusement machine market. From this time on the number of machines imported, primarily from Germany, increased every year. American made three reelers began to be imported again in limited quantities, mainly through the German exporting network. However, as in pre-war days this line of trade remained largely unadvertised. 1956 was to prove a turning point. In that year the government announced its intention of reforming the gaming laws, which it considered outdated. In the light of the Royal Commission's report of a few years' earlier (and favourable noises being made by people in the right quarters) expectations were raised as to the outcome of such reforms.

1956 was the year in which the first new, traditional format three reeler was advertised nationally, coming from an unexpected quarter, New South Wales in Australia. Within two years other machines began to be imported in increasing quantities, again from an unexpected quarter — Japan. These were made by the rapidly expanding firm of Sega, and were essentially copies of current Mills machines. The Japanese, and other German made copies eventually prompted the Mills Bell-O-Matic Corporation (now based in Nevada) to take out a full page advertisement in the World's Fair in June 1958 which asked: 'Are you getting genuine Mills Bells — or only imitations?' Indeed, as the decade drew to a close the number of new three reelers in circulation dramatically increased, although they were to prove little more than the vanguard of a huge influx of machines to Britain in the early 1960s following their legalisation.

The 1960 Betting and Gaming Act was in many ways a logical extension of the Royal Commission Report of ten years earlier, which in effect recognised the legitimacy of 'small time' gaming as a social activity free from the context of moral corruption or criminality. The 1960 Act effectively legalised gaming for profit, and as a consequence legitimised the use of the slot machine and other related games of chance. The three reeler was henceforth allowed to be used legally and on a national scale for the first time since its introduction almost half a century earlier, without fear of prosecution. As in Germany, its use was bounded by certain rational limitations which have since been modified and amended to suit prevailing conditions.

The legitimisation of the U.K. market led directly to the establishment of a number of indigenous companies devoted solely to the production of such machines. However, as important as some of these were to become their establishment came too late to effectively shift the balance of the world market in their favour. The 1960s were to see coin operated machines enter upon a new phase of their technological development, which by the end of the decade had made the mechanical marvels of yesteryear all but redundant.

The irony of the situation was perhaps best evidenced by the words of an old time operator, who when asked if he was happy with legitimisation after so many years of struggle, replied: "Certainly not! When they legalised the industry, they took all the fun out of the business."

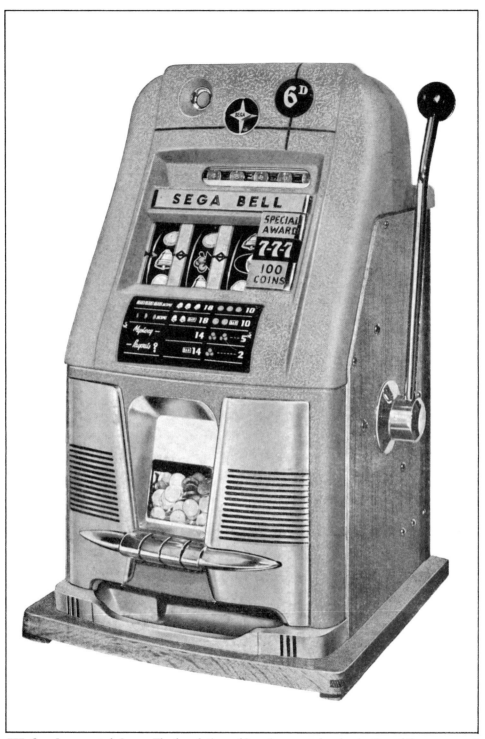

777: *Sega Incorporated, Japan. The foundations of Japan's present day domination of the amusement industry were laid in 1957 when the firm of Sega (with an initial workforce of only 3 men) began manufacturing copies of Mills Hightop machines.*

THE MACHINES

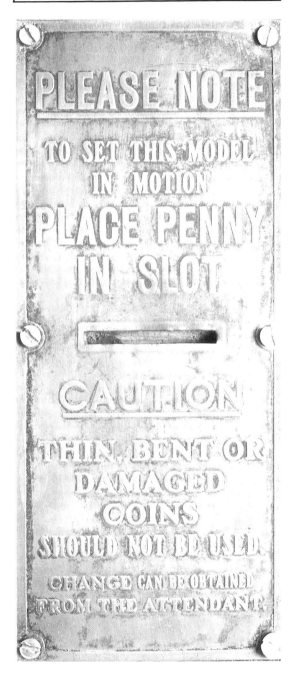

Advertising sheet: Caille Brothers Company, Detroit, 1902.

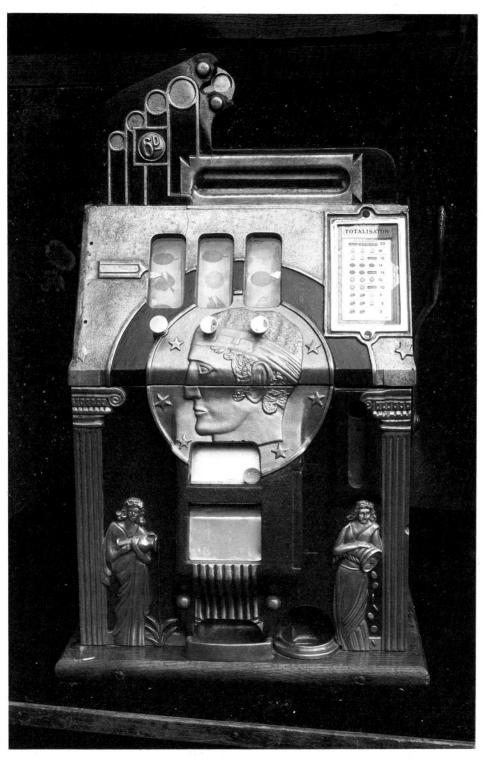

Silent Golden Bell (Roman Head): Mills Novelty Company, Chicago, 1932.

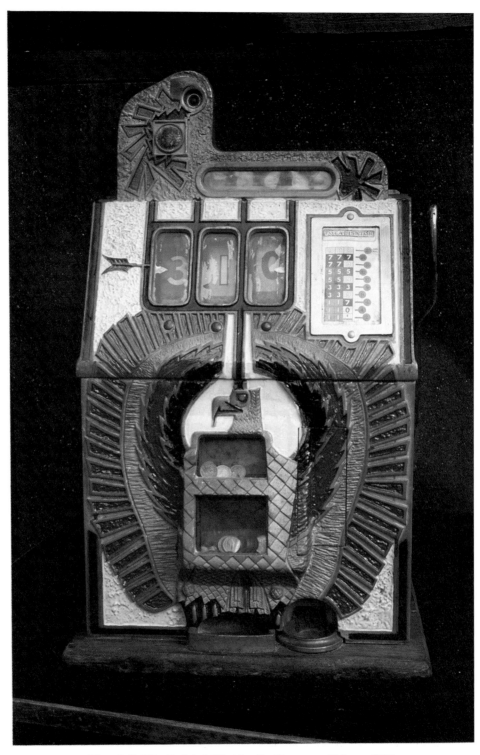

Silent Bell (War Eagle): Mills Novelty Company, Chicago, 1931.

'Egyptian' Bell: Maker uncertain. The manufacturer of one of the best designs of the 3 reeler ever made has yet to be ascertained.

Rol-a-Top: Watling Manufacturing Company, Chicago, 1935.

Full Team Football: Full Team Football Company, London, 1925.

Cricketer: Automatic Sports Company, London, 1903.

Yacht Racer: Automatic Sports Company, London, 1900.

Six Man Footballer: Automatic Sports Company, London, 1903.

Automatic Medical Electric Machine: J. Mason & Co., London, 1895.

The Racer: Doughty & Barrett, London, 1896.

Le Cochon Electriseur Automatique: Societe Generale Francaise D'Automatiques, Paris, c1898.

Imperial Electric Shock Machine: Imperial Electric Company, London, 1901.

Gypsy Fortune Teller: Automatic Amusement Company, London, 1889.

Fortune Teller: Maker unknown, c1895.

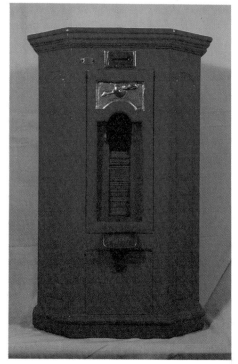

Chinese Crystal Gazer: Maker unknown, Blackpool, c1930.

Love Letter Box: Nelson Lee, Blackpool, c1900.

The Mysterious Hand (detail): Chas. Ahrens, London, 1930.

Musical Fairy (detail): John Dennison, Leeds, 1885.

Ticket Sorcerer (detail): John Dennison, Leeds, 1887.

1015: Rudolph Wurlitzer Manufacturing Company, New York, 1946.

Bottle Shooter: W. H. Ell & Company, London, c1904.

Krac Shot: W. H. Ell & Company, London, c1901.

Grip Tester: P. Everitt, London, 1889.

Strength Tester: R. Page, London, 1885.

Ajax Puncher: Caille Brothers Company, Detroit, c1904.

Negro Chocolate Vender: Maker unknown, c1895.

Elephant Chocolate Vender: Maker unknown, c1895.

Express Gold Changer: C. Garrett & Co., Birmingham, c1905.

Express Gold Changer: Express Gold Change Till Company, Birmingham, 1901.

Sentry Box Cigar Vender: Ludwig Stollwerck, Cologne, c1895.

Musical Cigar Vender: Maker unknown, Paris, c1887.

Kalloscope: Polyphon Musikwerke, Leipzig, c1895.

Poule Automatique: P. Leoni, Paris, 1897.

'Oh My' Negro Dancer: W. Hart, Kent, c1910.
(Revamp of Toy produced by Ernst Lehmann)

Mother Shipton: Argyle Automatic Company,
London, c1908.

119

Tivoli: Haydon & Urry, London, c1897 version.

Pickwick: H. Klein & Company, London, 1900.

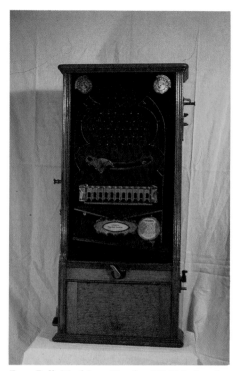

Fortuna: Automatic Skill Machines Company, London, 1901.

Four Ball Machine: Handan-Ni Ltd, London, 1913.

The Challenge: T. Flory, London, 1914.

Game of Skill: Price & Castell, London, 1899.

Bullseye: Cresset Coin Machine Company, Kent, 1909.

Success: New Polyphon Supply Co, Paris, 1910.

Allwin Reserve (with electric shock): Jentsch & Meerz, Leipzig, c1920.

Allies Flags: Automatic Novelty Company, London, 1916.

Pile ou Face: Bussoz, Paris, c1909.

Le Magic: P. Beraud, Paris, c1910.

Le Cannon: New Polyphon Supply Company, Paris, c1910.

Le Diabolique: P. Beraud, Paris, c1910.

Is Marriage a Failure?: J. Dennison, Leeds, 1890.

Haunted House Musical Automaton (detail): J. Dennison, Leeds, 1883.

CHAPTER SEVEN

Billiards And Pin Bagatelle

The classic, though highly erroneous story for the invention of the coin freed pin bagatelle game is often given as follows;

> Early in 1929, Mr. John J. Sloan, an advertising solicitor for 'Billboard' — which in those days catered to the carnival and circus trade, street vendors, and machine operators — observed an adaptation of bagatelle in the basement of his apartment building. The device had been built by a janitor for the amusement of his friends. Although the unknown, unsung inventor of the modern pintable utilised the traditional scoring objectives of bagatelle — holes or cups in a plane surface with the score value of each hole prominently displayed — he introduced 3 historic innovations: an inclined playfield; scoring holes partially surrounded by brass nails or pins; a spring loaded plunger . . . Mr. Sloan, intent on developing a new source of advertising revenue, described his subterranean discovery to several of his carnival equipment accounts, and one company In and Outdoor Games Inc built and marketed several coin operated bagatelle or pintables.

It doesn't really matter whether the events described in the story are true or not (Sloan might indeed have played a small part in the popularisation of coin freed bagatelle games at this time) since the claims made therein have absolutely no bearing upon reality. All of these so called 'new inventions' were already old hat by the late 1920s, indeed some of the elements were so old that their origins have been obscured by the passage of time.

The history of the bagatelle game is intimately linked to that of billiards, a game which appears to be of 15th century Italian origin. It is of significance however, that the names of both these games were to derive ultimately from French words (billiard signifying a cue, and bagatelle a trifle) since versions of both games were to enjoy enormous popularity at the court of Louis XIV of France in the 17th century.

The bagatelle board even in its earliest formats was to make use of holes or cups on the playing field, each of which would be ascribed a different value, and would be guarded by rows of pins or other objects. Such games were also additionally to feature items such as bells as the scoring objective. The 18th century was to witness the introduction of bagatelle boards and billiard tables to the public at large, so that by the last quarter of that century they were to be found in inns and taverns, particularly in Britain, as part of their stock in trade.

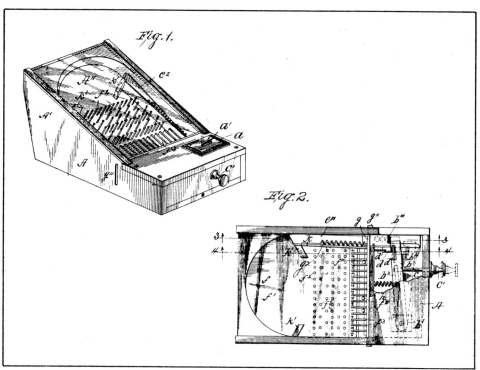

Patent Drawing for 'An Improved Coin Actuated Machine', Charles P. Young, Pennsylvania, 1893.

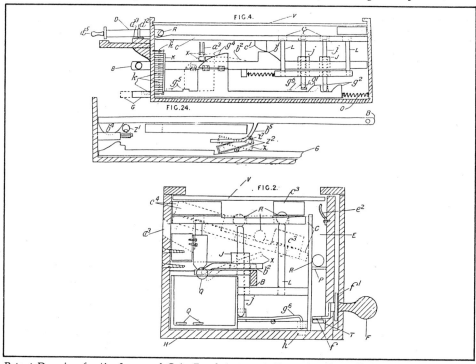

Patent Drawing for 'An Improved Coin Freed Automatic Repeating Bagatelle Machine for Delivery and Non Delivery of checks and Coins': Francis J. Cocks, Salop, U.K., 1901.

Companies were established during this period which devoted themselves solely to the manufacture of such items. Most notable of these is Thurstons in London, a company which still exists to this day. The popularity of such items in the 19th century was to remain as strong as ever. Witness the oft cited case from Dickens of members of the Pickwick Club (1836) 'beguiling their time' upon a bagatelle board in the Peacock Tavern. More notable evidence of such popularity can be inferred from the passing in Britain of the 1845 Gaming Act which hitherto expressly required the annual licensing of public billiard tables and bagatelle boards. The early 19th century was to see the introduction of a major new innovation to the playing of bagatelle, the spring loaded plunger, by means of which the ball (which had hitherto been propelled with a cue) could be shot up the playfield. Henceforth, bagatelle boards were to be found which made use of either system, although playing by means of a spring loaded plunger was to long remain subsidiary to playing by means of the more traditional cue.

The latter half of the 19th century was to see a vast increase in the manufacture of toys and toy appliances which in essence were to mirror the adult world. During this period, both bagatelle and billiards were to come within the scope of the toy manufacturer, and miniature versions of what had hitherto been adult games were to be manufactured. Significant in this context was to be the patenting in 1871 by Montague Redgrave, an American, of a table-top bagatelle game which encompassed almost all the key elements of the early pintable.

With the advent of coin freed appliances in the last quarter of the 19th century it was inevitable that such devices should come within the scope of the automatics industry. As early as 1878 in Britain, W.H. Tetley and S. Clayton were to patent a coin freed appliance 'for marking and scoring at billiards, Bagatelle, or other similar games, and for registering the number of games played.'

It was to be the first of a large variety of coin freed patents relating to billiard tables and bagatelle boards to be granted prior to the pintable boom of the early 1930s. However, the main emphasis during this early period was the automation of an already extant industry. Bagatelle had, almost since its inception, played second fiddle to the mighty game of Billiards. Billiard tables were to be more frequently encountered than bagatelle boards. In the late 19th and early 20th centuries Billiard Halls were established, catering solely to this perennially popular game as well as to its many variants such as Pool or Snooker. The bulk of the impetus at this time was therefore aimed at the automation of Billiards.

Having said this, bagatelle was also to find its niche. It too encompassed a host of variant games which, by and large, required a much smaller play area than that of billiards. Bagatelle related games had long since become part and parcel of the fairground. It was logical therefore, with the establishment of automatic arcades in the 1890s, that bagatelle should become an integral part of the scene with almost every established arcade prior to World War One including a bagatelle board or related game as part of its attractions. Although the bulk of such games were never automated, coin operated varieties were to be encountered early on. The credit for the

Haydon & Urry's
LATEST SENSATION—
AUTOMATIC BILLIARDS.

THE MOST NOVEL AND FASCINATING PENNY-IN-THE-SLOT GAME EVER INVENTED.

Exact model of Billiard Table, affording an ample scope for display of Skill and Judgment.

AN ENORMOUS ATTRACTION IN ANY SALOON.

Wanted at once, TWO THOUSAND positions for these Machines on Usual Terms.

Apply to THE ORIGINAL LICENSED VICTUALLERS' . . . . . . AUTOMATIC MACHINE PROVIDERS,

HAYDON & URRY, Limited,
353, Upper Street, Islington, LONDON, N.

Advertisement for: Automatic Billiards Machine, patented by Haydon & Urry Ltd, London, 1897.

first such device must go on present evidence to an American, Charles Young, who in 1893 took out a patent for a coin freed game of 'German Billiards'. It was to all intents and purposes the world's first 'pintable' — resembling in many ways the pinball games of the early 1930s.

The introduction of the miniaturised coin freed bagatelle game at this time was to have little impact in its own right upon the automatics market. There was, after all, a lot else going on. Like the coin operated kiddie ride of the early 1930s, it was destined to bide its time until the prevailing social climate was to favour its introduction on a mass scale. Having said this, the introduction in the early 1890s of bagatelle inspired gambling games, most notably in the form of the early European wall machines (which favoured a vertical as opposed to a horizontal playfield) was to have an immediate and marked impact upon the future course of the automatics industry.

That other miniaturised forms of bagatelle or billiards inspired games were to be produced during this period is attested to by a number of patents. In Britain in 1897 the firms of Haydon and Urry were to patent and market a small coin freed billiards game which featured a spring loaded plunger mounted on a universal joint, and gave a token or check for a successful shot. In 1901 F. J. Cocks patented a check payout bagatelle machine. In the United States in 1902 the Caille Brothers Company of Detroit were granted a patent for the Log Cabin — for long thought by collectors to have been the first coin freed pin bagatelle machine. The intervening years were to see the granting of something in excess of twenty-five patents relating to coin freed billiards or bagatelle games, presenting us thereby with a picture very much at variance with that given in the John Sloan story.

That the late 1920s and early 1930s were to see the beginnings of a pinball boom is without doubt. Starting tentatively in America in the late 1920s, it was to turn in a few short years into a craze which was to sweep across the western world. It is hard for many of us today to understand the impact that the pinball machine was to make, particularly when they are confronted with some of the most successful of the products of this time — essentially nothing more than tacky little boxes spattered with pins and a few holes, and containing virtually no mechanism. Yet sweep the world they did, leaving a whole new generation of cash rich companies in their wake. For example, both the Ballyhoo (launched by the Bally Manufacturing Company in December 1931) and the Baffle Ball (launched by D. Gottlieb and Company in January 1932) were to reach production totals in the region of 50,000 machines apiece in less than two years of production.

The success of these games at this time was dependent upon two key factors. Firstly they were cheap to produce, and were therefore sold cheaply ($16 and $17.50 respectively) enabling many thousands of hitherto unemployed people to set up in business as pintable operators. In some parts of America even the Church was to become involved, with local priests providing the capital necessary for the purchase of such items by unemployed parishioners! Secondly, because they were initially used solely as games of skill with little or no gambling element, their public use was more palatable to the authorities.

Log Cabin, Caille Brothers Company, 1901.

Monorail Skittle Alley, New Polyphon Supply Company, London, c1910.

Seven Arches, Handan-Ni Ltd, London, 1919.

132

Bally Hoo: Bally Manufacturing Corporation, Chicago, 1932.

Wings: Rock-Ola Manufacturing Corporation, Chicago, 1933.

Goldrush (payout): Rock-Ola Manufacturing Corporation, Chicago, 1935.

Sportsman (payout): O. D. Jennings & Company, Chicago, 1934.

Humpty Dumpty: D. Gottlieb & Company, Chicago, 1947.

Any game which seemingly offers a player a cash based return for his efforts greater than the amount of money originally staked is ultimately seen to be more desirable by the player. It will as a consequence enjoy repeat play over a greater period of time. The less time the game takes to play, the greater the potential return for the operator. It was inevitable therefore that these basic principles of human nature would within a short space of time be incorporated into the playing of pin games. By the middle 1930s many models were to feature but a single ball, as opposed to the original ten, a high score resulting in an automatic payout in cash or tokens. This primary development of the pintable during the 1930s was to be coupled with a host of other electrically based innovations designed to give greatly enhanced player appeal. It is a little understood fact, that had the pingame of the 1930s been left solely to its own devices it would have ultimately developed into a full blown gambling game. The increasing censure of the authorities in the late 1930s and 1940s was to steer it back onto its initial course as a game to be played solely for entertainment.

It is ironic perhaps, that although the peak years of the pinball craze were to be those of the 1930s (which witnessed the marketing and manufacture of a plethora of such games on both sides of the Atlantic, as well as a host of important innovations in game design and technology) the pinball machine as we now know it was essentially a post WWII product. The key development was the introduction of the flipper. Although similar devices had been marketed in the years prior to the outbreak of World War Two, the flipper as a key element in the playing of pinball was not to be widely encountered until after the marketing of a machine called Humpty Dumpty in November 1947 by D Gottlieb and Company. It was an innovation that was to be immediately copied by all the other leading manufacturers of pinball machines.

The severe legal restrictions placed upon coin operated machines in the early 1950s, particularly in the United States (which had achieved a world manufacturing hegemony of coin freed devices by this time) was to ensure that the pintable as an entertainment game was to survive and prosper throughout the next two decades, becoming thereby one of the mainstays of the modern amusement industry until the coming of the video game in the early 1970s.

Before closing however, let us momentarily return to the heady days of the 1930s and pay our due respects to Mrs Mildred Worden of Beaumont, Texas, who in the summer of 1935 sued her husband for divorce. Her marriage had irretrievably broken down, she told the court, her husband no longer loved her, and as with all classic divorce cases there was a third party. To pile shame onto misery her husband had been caught on a number of occasions 'in flagrante delecto' his arms around the one he loved. . Yes indeed dear reader, the humble pintable had achieved the ultimate — it had seduced Mr. Worden!

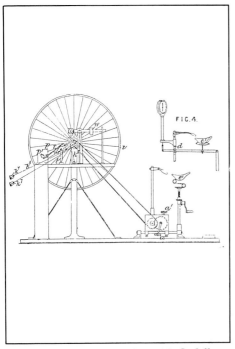

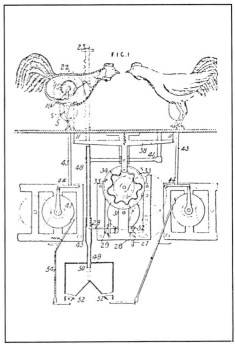

Patent: 'Speed Testing Appliance,' J. C. Sellars, London, 1887.

Patent: 'Improvements in Coin Operated Automatons,' Arthur M. Pierce, Brooklyn, New York, 1889.

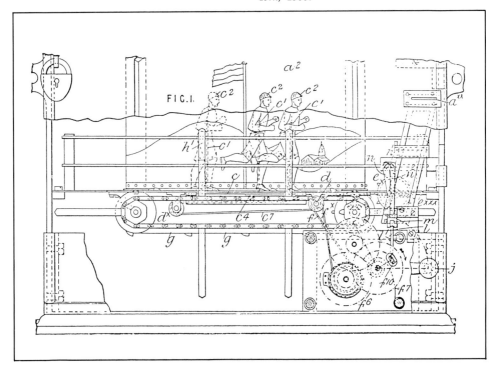

Patent: 'Improvements in Mechanical Toys,' Cornelis F. A. Roell, London, 1891.

136

CHAPTER EIGHT
Competitive Games

A coin freed competitive game may be broadly described as one in which a player is required to perform an act of skill or prowess upon a machine either on his own or in competition with another player, the prime purpose being one of entertainment or amusement rather than gambling. In its broadest sense it is a definition which can encompass a very wide spectrum of coin freed devices. In its narrower sense it is applicable primarily to games which seek to mimic other sporting pastimes with one player competing directly against another.

This particular genre has its origins in a number of machines patented during the late 1880s and early 1890s deriving from different sections of the coin freed spectrum, most notably gambling games and strength testers. Many of the early gambling games were to make use of animated figures which sought to mimic a race or some other sporting activity, the player's objective being to determine in advance which of the figures would be the winning one. As we have noted in an earlier chapter, the earliest of these, a horse racing game, was patented in Britain by William Oliver in 1887. In subsequent years it was to prove a very popular gambling game format. The 1890s in particular were to see a great increase in the sophistication and technical virtuosity of such devices. Although horse racing machines were to be the most commonly encountered of the animated gambling games, they were in essence to be but one of a number of different and very novel formats. In America, for instance, as early as 1889 Arthur Pierce patented a game which featured fighting cocks. However, the person to whom the greater part of the credit for the popularisation and subsequent proliferation of such sporting games, must go to a man named Cornelis Roell, a Dutch jonkheer, resident in London during the early 1890s. He was to be granted a whole wad of patents relating to a number of very unusual machines which were to feature amongst other figures: animated boxers, athletes, and horse riders.

We can now turn to another important aspect of competitive games, direct participation on the part of the player. Although virtually all the strength or athletic machines fall within this broad category, the most important devices in this context were to be the speed testers. The earliest patent for a coin freed speed tester was granted to J.C. Sellars in 1887. On this particular contraption the player was required to sit upon something resembling a disembowelled bicycle and to pedal for all he was worth. A gauge at the front would register the maximum speed attained. By 1893 the principle had been applied to animated games. In March of that year J.G. Cumming, an important pioneer of early arcade games, patented a wall mounted horse racing machine. It featured two horses, one of which was controlled by a clockwork motor whilst the other was controlled directly by the player by means of a crank situated at the front of the machine. If the player's horse reached the winning post first his coin would be returned to him. In 1895 a London based fairground automaton maker, George De Melven patented a multiple player game in which figures (later versions would feature monkeys) were made to clamber up poles by means of cranks

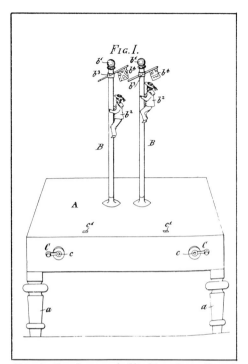

Patent: 'An Improved Climbing Race Game,' George de Melven, London, 1895.

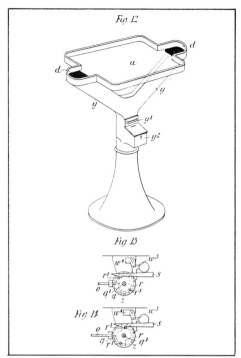

Patent: 'A Coin Freed Game-Playing Apparatus,' Graydon Poore, London, 1893.

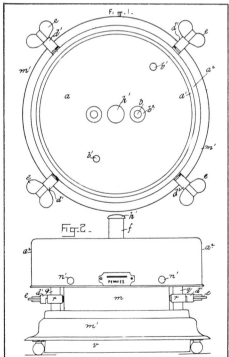

Patent: 'A New Game and Apparatus Appertaining Thereto,' Charles M. Linley, London, 1896.

Cycle Racer: Palmers Automatic Machine Syndicate, Birmingham, 1899.

operated by the players.

The year 1896 was to see the introduction of two notable machines. The first of these was patented by T.W. Doughty and C.A. Barrett. It was a small countertop, two player, horse racing game. Each player would crank a handle in order to move his horse along a track. It required two pennies to play, the winner being rewarded by the return of his coin. In the same year Ernest Mathewson, the pioneering proprietor of what was shortly to become the Automatic Sports Company of London, patented the Two Man Footballer. The original version of this game was housed in a small wooden cabinet. It contained the figures of two footballers each situated in front of his respective goal. The two competing players would press down upon a trigger in order to make the legs of the two mannikins kick out at a ball. A goal in the opponents net would secure the return of the winning player's coin.

Although animated figures were to prove amongst the most popular elements of the competitive game, machines were to be made which dispensed with them altogether. Two keys games which fit into this latter category were to be marketed during the course of the 1890s. The first of these was patented by Graydon Poore in 1893. It made use of a flat, glass topped, playing surface. Situated upon the playing surface were two goals, one at either end, and two pivoted knockers or bats. Insertion of a coin would release a ball which the players attempted to hit into the opponents goal. In 1896 Charles Linley patented a game which consisted of a circular, glass topped, playing surface. The players goals (essentially holes in the playing surface) were situated just off centre. The entire playing surface was pivoted, the players attempting to manipulate the ball into their opponent's goal by slanting or tilting the surface by means of a system of rack and pinions. The ready popularity of such games, particularly the horse racer and the footballer, was to ensure the incorporation of competitive games into the pantheon of the automatics industry. By the early 1900s the range of two player sporting games had widened considerably to include: tugs of war, cycle racers, rowing boats, boxers, table tennis players (the game of Ping Pong enjoyed an enormous vogue at this time), and even swimmers racing in a tank of water!

If surviving numbers are anything to go by the machines marketed by the Automatic Sports Company in the early 1900s were to be amongst the most popular, remaining in production up until the early 1920s. From about 1900 onwards they were to be manufactured in ornate cast iron cases. In 1899 the Two Man Footballer was to be complemented by the marketing of the Two Man Cricketer.

In 1900 a Yacht Racer was added, the yachts floating in a tank of water. (The originator of this type of game was R.E. Wickes who patented a single player Navigation machine a year earlier). In 1903 the company introduced a Six Man Footballer, essentially a more refined version of their earlier game, although credit for the first football game to incorporate more than two figures must go to a machine patented by R.H. and J.F. Shaw in 1898. In subsequent years (1912 onwards) the range of machines was to be enhanced by the addition of the Golf game, as well as a variety of shooting games.

The Knockout: London Automatic Machine Company, London, 1922.

Headball: London Automatic Machine Company, London, 1926.

Steer a Boat: Chas. Ahrens, London, 1928.

Huntsmans Derby: Chas. Ahrens, London, c1930.

140

Marathon Cycle Racer: Chas. Ahrens, London, 1930.

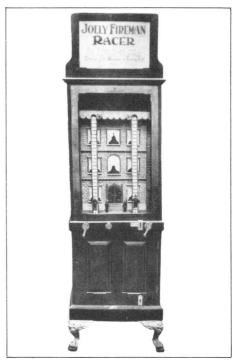

Jolly Fireman Racer: Chas. Ahrens, London, 1927.

Pushball: L. Walton & Co., Blackpool, 1925.

Great Polo Game: London Automatic Machine Company, London, c1927.

The Bar: L. Walton & Co., Blackpool, 1929.

Much has been made of Mathewson's work in recent years owing to the survival rate of his company's machines as well as to the ornate cast iron cabinets in which they are contained. He was indeed one of the most successful of the early manufacturers of arcade games. Yet from a historical point of view it should be borne in mind that he did not work in a vacuum. There were many other competitors whose machines have not survived the years in great number, but who must be given equal (and in some instances greater) credit for the invention and popularisation of these highly entertaining devices.

The 1920s were to see yet another wave of invention and innovation relating to coin freed competitive games. Having declined in popularity during the years of the First World War, they were to be given a new lease of life during the 1920s and 30s following the introduction of large free standing cabinet versions. The instigator of this new wave was to be George Barr, who in 1921 patented the first Full Team Football machine, which incorporated two complete teams of mannikins, each resplendent in a little knitted jersey and kicking leg. George Barr and his brother Harry (who incidentally hated the sight of each other in later years) had long since been engaged in the manufacture of coin freed machines. They are little known today owing to the fact that they concentrated their efforts upon the manufacture of machines to order for other better known companies, who would then market them under their own name.

The Full Team Football was to be an instant success. Copies or versions of it were to be marketed by other manufacturers up until the outbreak of the Second World War. As a consequence of the success of this machine the 1920s and 30s were to spawn a whole host of large free standing competitive games encompassing a diversity of sporting and novel themes, such as golf, cricket, boxing, horse racing, greyhound racing, and even a race to see which of two players could fill up a pint glass of beer! Although by this time, following the introduction of three reel gambling games, the American hegemony of the automatics industry had been virtually assured, it is a little known fact that it is to the British manufacturers of the 1920s and earlier that the Americans must pay homage for the introduction of such competitive games to their domestic market.

The popularity of competitive games was to remain constant, with post war manufacturers introducing updated versions. They were to remain part of the stock in trade of arcades, particularly at British seaside resorts, up until the 1960s.

Before closing, let us pay our respects to a machine promoted by the International Mutoscope Company of New York in 1933. It was hailed as a new device featuring (believe it or not) racing cockroaches! According to the company's president, William Rabkin, demand for the devices was great, although they were unable to obtain enough trained cockroaches to send out the machines. He explained: 'A special breed is needed to make the races interesting, and a wide search is being made for the right kind.' It makes one wonder however, if one of these charming little creatures ever crawled out of the machine, who would win? The cockroach, or the punter fleeing for the exit?

"OLD SONG."

"I'm poor Sailor Jack,
　Just come home from Sea,
With 'Shiners' in my sack—
　What do you think of me?"

I can Electrify you by the Profits I make ! !

Splendid

Casting.

Well

Decorated.

Suitable for

either

indoors or

outdoors.

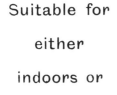

Powerful

Current

regulated at

will.

Electricity

is

Life !

"When I wink, it DOES YOU GOOD" !

PRICE - - £8 - 0 - 0

Advertisement for Electric Sailor: Polyphon Musikwerke, Leipzig, c1910.

CHAPTER NINE

Electric Shock Machines

> Hundreds, perhaps thousands, have received unspeakable good; and I have not known one man, woman, or child, who has received any hurt thereby; so that when I hear any talk of the danger of being electrified (especially if they are medical men who talk so), I cannot but impute it to great want either of sense or honesty.
>
> We know that it is a thousand medicines in one; in particular, that it is the most efficacious medicine in nervous disorders of every kind, which has ever yet been discovered.

These sentiments were expressed by no less a person than the great evangelist John Wesley in the late 1700s. It must come as a surprise to many to learn just how old electric shock devices are. Their history essentially begins with the invention of the Leyden Jar in Holland in 1745. In its original form it consisted of a jar partly filled with water with the opening at the neck stopped with a cork, through which a wire or nail was pushed so that its end dipped in the water. The jar was charged by means of a friction machine connected to the free end of the wire or nail protruding out of the top of the bottle. Subsequent touching of the jar would result in an appreciable electric shock.

Within a short space of time Leyden Jars were being used for medical purposes, the electric shock they gave being pronounced as an almost universal panacea. From the late 1750s onward a number of special clinics were established in the major European capitals. London alone could boast five such places. Electricity, and in particular electrical treatment became the wonder of the age.

Although the Leyden Jar was the first publicly used shocking device (we can discount Benjamin Franklin's kite flying experiment of 1752, in spite of what it did for the advancement of mankind, since it had an unnerving tendency to electrocute the user), it was soon to be joined by other frictional shocking machines. In 1782 in Britain, Edward Mairne was granted a patent for an insulated medical electrical machine, comprising a central glass cylinder with a friction pad which was flanked by two brass conductors. Leads from the conductors were applied to the patient's body, with supposedly beneficial results. By the late 1700s any doctor worth his salt considered electrical therapy as an indispensable adjunct to his trade.

In 1787 for example, Dr. St. Clair reported of his success in curing no less than twenty-four hysterical people in Lancashire by means of his portable electric machine. In 1804 the Swedish chemist Jac Berzelius received a doctor's degree in medicine for his dissertation on the use of electricity to cure illness. By the 1830s a number of instrument makers had begun

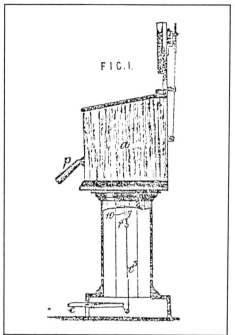

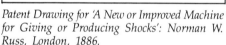

Patent Drawing for 'A New or Improved Machine for Giving or Producing Shocks': Norman W. Russ, London, 1886.

Corinthian Electro-Medical Battery: Electro-Medical Battery Company Ltd., London, 1888.

the manufacture of small hand driven generators in which the current was conducted to two handles which the patient grasped firmly, the higher the voltage generated the greater the effect. Makers as a consequence experimented with ways of varying the voltage, including different ways of winding the coils and ways to short circuit the magnetic field to a higher or lower degree with a magnetic shunt. These were the first electrical machines to go into large scale production.

The key development, in so far as we are concerned, was the invention of the induction coil. Although originally invented in America by Charles Page in 1836, it was not to be found in common usage until after its reinvention and improvement by Heinrich Ruhmkorff in France in 1851. In practice, an induction coil is a special form of transformer which when coupled with a battery converts an ordinary direct current at low voltage into an intermitenent current at high voltage. By means of the induction coil, voltages of up to 1,000 volts could be obtained in graduated stages from an input voltage (in the form of a battery) of only 6 volts. Strong stuff, but for electro-medical usage, the output voltage was limited to 50-100 volts.

By the latter half of the 19th century electric shock devices had inevitably become part of the travelling showman's repetoire, Either as universal panaceas, or as entertaining sideshow attractions whereby the patrons were invited, upon payment of a small fee, to touch or shake hands with suitably insulated 'electric' ladies, or seat themselves upon 'electric' chairs.

As can now be readily seen, by the time coin operated versions of such machines came onto the market, beginning in 1886, such devices in various

146

guises had been in use for well over a century, so that in this respect they were not fundamentally new inventions.

Coupled with the introduction of automatic electric shock machines was the introduction of a plethora of related devices designed for home use, which were to have a great vogue in late 19th century society. They ranged from straightforward electro-medical machines through to more exotic counterparts such as electric combs, belts, corsets, and even footwear.

Where the coin operated machines scored was that they were able to facilitate the use of electric shock devices for the first time by the public at large, the vast majority of whom could not afford to pay for doctors, or buy the necessary equipment. Such machines, after vending and weighing machines, were to be perhaps the most commonly encountered coin operated device in the late 1800s, as evidenced by the large number of patents granted for such machines during this period.

The first British patent for a coin operated electric shock machine was granted to Norman Willis Russ in July 1886, although this chronological distinction was probably due more to accident rather than innovative foresight on the part of Russ, since even he had to admit in his patent application that "it has already been broadly proposed to obtain electric shocks by similar means" (i.e. coin operated). Before 1886 had run its full course a further eight patents had been granted to other inventors, and by 1890 the tally had reached thirty. Included amongst these patentees were a number of the successful pioneers of the coin-op genre: William Oliver (July 1886) — his machine gave a printed card showing the shock received and rang a bell if a certain voltage was achieved; Percival Everitt (August 1886 and November 1887) - the latter included a visual display; Mortimer Justin (October 1886) — his machine incorporated a clockwork time limiting device, important to the money conscious operator in that it stopped the user from 'hogging' the machine; Joseph Mason (January 1889 and November 1890) — the latter retating to a cigarette vending attachment for delivering a cigarette to the user if he withstood a certain amount of shock.

Many of the earliest electric shock machines were to be relatively large, freestanding affairs, which required the patron to stand on a platform in order to make them operate. However, they soon developed into countertop or wall mounted devices comprising two handles and a dial. The user inserted a coin, grasped the handles, and slowly turned one of them. This gradually increased the electric shock, which was registered on the dial. Although the induction coil was to predominate, a few machines were made which incorporated related technology, most notably in the form of Geissler tubes.

Great play was made of their medical properties, even when in later years they had been largely discredited by the medical profession. Under the almost universal logo of 'Electricity is Life' they were to claim the ability to cure such diverse illnesses as 'Nervousness, Rheumatism, Neuritis, Lumbago, Neuralgia and Sciatica.' This health giving aspect was enhanced in a number of ways. Shock machines were combined with strength testers or, as in the case of an 1890 patent, with a weighing machine and lung tester (which incorporated a gambling element in the form of a coloured

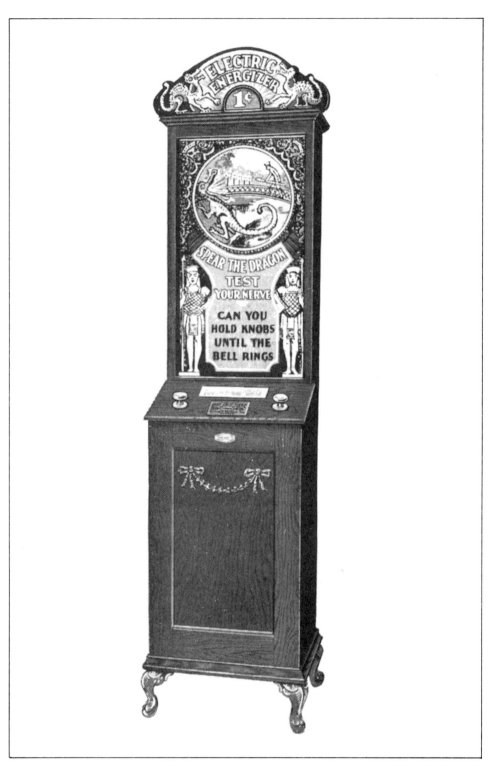

Electric Energiser: Exhibit Supply Company, Chicago, c1929.

spinning disc with pictures of racehorses on its periphery).

The outward appearance of machines was designed to enhance their life preserving role. A few were made to resemble Greek temples, most notably the Corinthian patented by T.W. Ford in 1888, and the Electro-Medical Battery patented by Joseph Mason a year later. For many, as with other areas of the coin-op genre, novelty was to play a key role. The year 1888 saw the patenting of a coin operated electric chair — an idea which by January 1889 was to have more sinister connotations, following its adoption by the State of New York as a means of executing criminals. In 1890 came the first zoomorphic machine which was made, surprisingly, in the shape of a kangaroo. Inserting a coin, and holding the paws whilst pressing one of them down would achieve the desired result.

Unhappily none of these charming machines are known to survive, although a later version in the form of a miniature sailor has survived. So too has the Electric Pig made by the French pioneering firm of Maurice and Molle in the late 1890s. However, in this instance trotter manipulation is out. He sits upright on his haunches, with two handles protruding from his stomach. It is these you grasp, and he seems to like it, if the grin on his face is anything to go by! (The pig, in France, is a symbol of good luck). Other machines were to incorporate moving figures, the earliest form of which dates from 1890, one of which caused a little figure with a lighted head to dance; the more the shock, the greater the dance.

Later machines were to incorporate a specific task for the player, whereby a bicycle or car was made to move up an inclined track as in J. Jofeh's machine of 1902, or a man with a spear was made to move towards a dragon as in the Exhibit Supply Company's Electric Energiser of the 1920s.

The heyday of the electric shock machine was essentially in the years prior to the 1914-18 war, although such devices appeared in ever diminishing numbers (apart from a brief vogue in the States in the mid 1930s) continuing to be made up until the 1940s.

In Europe they were to be incorporated, as we have seen in an earlier chapter, into gambling games as a means of by-passing anti-gambling legislation, and in this form they were manufactured from 1914 up until the late 1920s. The increasing use of more hazardous electrical gadgetry in the home increased the public's awareness of its potential harm. This was fostered by media reports of electrocution from mains electricity and ultimately relegated electro-medical devices to the more 'lunatic' fringes of the medical profession. Even in the early 1950s some manufacturers of electrically operated games felt obliged to reassure the public that there was no danger playing their machines, with 'No electricity! No shocks!' written on the front of them.

However, a distinction between mains electricity and the electric shocks given by machines must be drawn. Whereas a shock from mains voltage, if not enough to kill, is at the very least equivalent to a hefty kick from a size ten boot in the small of the back, the shock from an electric shock machine is more a tingling sensation, the muscles tighten, and one leaves feeling light headed.

Electric Volta: D. Harper & Co., London, 1899.

Electron: New Polyphon Supply Company, London, c1905.

Haydon Premier: W. Haydon & Co., London, 1902.

Simplex: Caille Brothers Company, Chicago, c1902.

Volta: Jentsch & Meerz, Leipzig, 1920.

Before closing, let us take a salutory note of the following anecdote pertaining to the Mills Novelty Company of Chicago, in its heyday in the early 1930s, at that time run by H.S. Mills' sons. Being young, wealthy, and relatively carefree, they liked to live life to the full, part of which was evidenced by the practical jokes they played on their guests. On this occasion, before a celebratory banquet, all the guests' chairs had been suitably wired up. After the guests had arrived, and each had duly taken their allocated seat, a switch (placed at the top end of the table) was discreetly flicked. Needless to say, the guests immediately rose to the occasion amidst shrieks of surprise and howls of laughter. All that is except one, a woman, who calmly kept her seat, wondering what on earth was going on. As the laughter died down, all eyes turned on her. Her dreadful secret was out . . . she was wearing rubber knickers!

The Eye the Window of the Soul: Argyle Automatic Company, London, 1908 version.

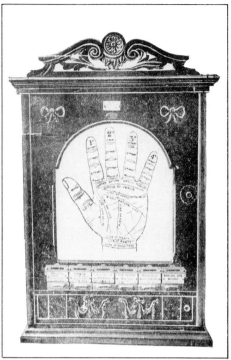

Hand Palmistry: Argyle Automatic Company, London, 1908 version.

New Photography: Argyle Automatic Company, London, 1908 version.

Whirlygig: Maker unknown, Germany, c1900.

152

CHAPTER TEN
Fortune Tellers

Mechanisation of the art of divination, in the form of casting lots, or more specifically in the form of a wheel turning, can be traced back to distant times. Man has since his earliest days endeavoured to discover the future course of his life and the interpretation of chance or random events has always played a large part in this process. In the ancient world a number of goddesses were represented in association with a wheel. Most notable of these is the Roman goddess Fortuna, who was depicted as a steated figure on a wheel, most often in the form of a statuette or a coin impression.

Fortuna's wheel was seen as representing the various stages of a man's life, both good and bad. The notion of a 'wheel of fortune' whose random spinning would determine the future course of events was a deep rooted one, and its depiction can be found in many diverse cultures. In particular, three dimensional representations of such a wheel were to be a common sight in medieval churches. They were hung up on the roofs of churches and worked by means of a rope, and were regarded by many as an oracle.

In more modern times, particularly in the 19th century, such wheels were to be found in use at country fairs and fairgrounds across Europe, where they were used not only as a means of telling fortunes, but also as gambling games. Gambling and fortune telling are inextricably linked through the phenomenon of chance. As a consequence, many of the earliest coin operated fortune telling machines were to draw upon the principle of a spinning or turning wheel for their operation.

Fortune telling was to be automated very early on in the history of the coin freed machine. A few years before 1820 (the precise year has not been determined) the famous Swiss automaton maker, Jean David Maillardet, made his Great Magician Clock. Strictly a 'one off', it took the form of a large mantlepiece clock, seated above which was the figure of a magician, in long robes and pointed hat. When a small enamel tablet bearing a question was placed into a little drawer at the top of the machine, the wizard would stand up, roll his eyes, and wave his magic wand towards a little mirror above his head. Shutters would then open to reveal the answer. If the drawer was shut without the correct type of tablet being inserted a death's head would appear. Many years later, when the first coin freed fortune telling patent was granted, in 1867 to J. Parkes, a similar format was to be adopted. A disc with a question written on it was inserted into the machine, which would then cause a shutter to open, thus revealing an answer. Both these machines were very much exhibition pieces that could not be effectively left unattended.

However, it is to these exhibition pieces that one must essentially turn to find some of the earliest examples of the coin-op principle. As we have already noted in an earlier chapter, the 1850s through to the 1870s were to be the 'gestation' period of coin freed machines. That they were produced in a fairly wide variety is without doubt, yet relatively little has as yet been unearthed concerning these early machines, primarily because very few were ever designed to be marketed or produced in any quantity. (The one exception was to be in the case of mechanical banks which were designed in the main for home, as opposed to public use). The bulk of such machines during this period appear to have been built as 'one offs', produced to satisfy the immediate needs of their makers, and as a result the majority of such pieces were to be encountered by the public at large only on display at set exhibitions, and not, as in the later period, on the streets, or in the diverse shops, or railway stations of the great metropolises.

One such maker, of whom a little is known, was John Dennison of Leeds, who from 1875 onwards regularly exhibited his machines (most of which were coin operated) at bazaars, fetes, and exhibitions across the north of England. All were to take the form of working models, some of them given an additional function in that they were designed to tell the user's fortune.

The earliest of these was perhaps the Musical Fairy, the original version of which was to be exhibited in the late 1870s. A series of numbered questions were displayed at the top of the machine. The player turned a pointer at the front of the machine to the number of the question he wanted to ask. He inserted a coin, which set a cylinder music box in motion, and animated the figure of a fairy situated at the front right hand side of the machine. The fairy would turn and raise her hand and one of two shutters at the back of the machine would move aside to reveal the answer to the player's question.

Another model was the Ticket Fairy, the original of which was in use prior to 1882. This model incorporated two moving figures, but had no musical accompaniment. The figures would turn towards a mirror situated at the back of the machine, whilst an ingenious delivery mechanism would automatically deliver to the player a card bearing his fortune. Both of these machines were to prove very popular, and although never mass produced (each model was painstakingly hand built) were to be made in a number of different versions over the next decade or so. Miraculously, versions of both these machines have survived the years, complete with original clockwork mechanism, and animated figures. However, since almost none of the machines of this period were to be patented the extant records remain by and large silent.

Indeed, it is not until 1889 that one encounters the first patent relating to a coin freed fortune telling machine designed to be exploited on a mass scale. This was granted to Anthony Harris, and took the much simpler form of a wall mounted cabinet incorporating a spinning dial. It was to be marketed in two versions. The first, as we have noted, in the form of a fortune teller, the disc bearing a chromolithographed portrait of a gypsy, and sold appropriately enough as the Gypsy Fortune Teller. The second version took the form of a gambling game bearing a different chromolithographed disc, the awards being paid out manually depending upon where the disc stopped. No versions of the latter machine are known to survive.

The year 1889 was also to witness the patenting of an automatic machine which literally told the player his fortune, by means of a phonograph. The late 1880s and early 1890s were to witness a vogue for a wide variety of coin operated 'talking' machines which were to prove many years ahead

X-Ray Photography: British Manufacturing Company, London, c1925 version.

Astrologer: British Manufacturing Company, London, c1925 version.

Gipsy: British Manufacturing Company, London, c1925 version.

Heaven & Hell: Bollands Amusement Machine Supply Company, London, 1952 version.

Eric: Original Machine Manufacturers, Southend, 1936.

Electric Crystal Gazer: Coin Operating Company, Birmingham, 1931.

Scientific Automatic Palmistry: Chas. Ahrens, London, 1932.

The Great occultos: Chas. Ahrens, London, 1921.

of their time. Owing to the relatively primitive state of the art at the time of their first introduction, all such devices were to have an early demise and it was to be many years before the technology was available to make them truly feasible.

In 1891 the first card delivery fortune tellers were marketed. They took the form of a simple wall mounted cabinet, comprising a series of drawers, each of which vended a card printed with a fortune ostensibly determined from one of a number of physiological characteristics of the user, such as the colour of his hair, the colour of his eyes, or even the shape of his nose! Early pioneers in this field were to be S.D.S. Ross and J.R. Hughes. Over the ensuing decades literally hundreds of different types of card delivery fortune telling machines were to be marketed. Indeed, since each of these machines was basically the same (the only essential difference being the number of drawers and slots incorporated, ranging in number from one to twelve), it was a relatively simple process to market a new model. So intense was the· competition in this area, that one leading British manufacturer of fortune telling machines in the early 1900s advertised a £100 guarantee of authenticity for the fortunes dispensed by his machines.

More ostentatious versions of the 1890s and early 1900s were to incorporate charming little figures that were either stationary decorations of a set piece scene (such as a gypsy encampment), or which moved (hands, eyes, or lips) each time the drawer was pulled out. By the late 1890s independent clockwork figures were to be commonly found which, like the earlier Dennison's, appeared to animate the card delivery procedure. As the new century progressed a number of these automatons had grown in size, so much so that by the outbreak of the First World War they were to be found, life size, in large free standing cabinets. After insertion of a coin the figure (more commonly that of a gypsy) would go through the motions of 'determining' a person's fortune before delivering his card. They were to remain a perenially popular feature of arcades over the course of the 20th century. So popular were they in fact that even large department stores sited them; Woolworth's for example, were to operate a number of fortune tellers in the years prior to the outbreak of World War Two.

However, the arm of the law was to reach even into this seemingly innocuous area of the automatics industry. In 1910, advertisements such as the following started appearing in the press:

> Have an interesting letter written by the unseen hand of the Gypsy Queen on plain paper. In English or German. The quickest and best money getter for the Seaside, Parks, Fairs is the Gypsy Queen. I have made 750 Pounds in 3 seasons, you can do likewise. A Gypsy Queen with 1,000 papers costs only £5/10/0d. I have got a new lot of invisible fortunes showing the impression of the palm of the respective persons hands, showing the life, head and heart line, including a long reading, 12/- per 1,000. I am showing figures in the Manchester Chronicle and Industrial Exhibition in Manchester and they are the only novelties taking 2d a time. — O Friedman, 115 Bignor Street, Hightown, Manchester.

CUPID'S POST OFFICE

A CONTINUAL source of innocent and pleasing amusement. The popularity of the Cupid is as old as the song "I Got a Letter From My Love." Whether young or old—men, women and children never pass by without paying Cupid for one of his cleverly written love messages. The machine represents a post office with real letters arranged in the boxes. Cupid sits back of the window ready to hand out a love token to men from one side and to women from the other side. There are 24 assorted love letters for men and 24 for women—arranged consecutively—something different each time. On each letter is a photograph of the sweetheart sender. On the reverse side a printed fortune—a great big penny's worth. This machine is fitted with our famous Exhibit patented sliding slots and with metal card compartments. Cabinet handsomely finished in natural oak. Ornaments brightly colored papier mache and aluminum castings. Machine can be had either with or without the base cabinet. Enough letters are included free with each machine to pay back the cost.

Floor Model with 12,500 free cards $125.00
Counter Model with 11,000 free cards $110.00
Reorders of cards $2.50 per thousand
DIMENSIONS: Height 7 feet; width 29 inches; depth 11 inches; weight 93 pounds.

Cupids Post Office: Exhibit Supply Company, Chicago, c1929.

Gypsy Queens, which as the advertisement implies, were to become all the rage, were not coin operated, but took the form of a life size automaton with moving eyes. A player would pay the operator his 1d or 2d and receive a seemingly blank piece of paper on which he would sign his name. The operator would then place the paper in the Gypsy Queen's pocket and with great show would ask her to reveal the player's fortune. A few moments later the operator would take out the same scrap of paper, and lo and behold, in addition to the player's signature would be his fortune dutifully written by the mysterious hand of the Gypsy! In fact these seemingly blank pieces of paper had already been written on with invisible ink, which a quantity of sulphate of potash contained within the gypsy's pocket would make visible. The illusion proved to be too effective, and very soon operators of such automatons across the country were to be found up before the courts charged with 'professing to tell fortunes' contrary to the Vagrancy Act of 1824. Convictions, and there were many, invariably meant a fine or imprisonment.

As a consequence all 'guarantees' of the veracity of fortunes dispensed by automatic machines were hastily withdrawn, and the little ditties which were to be found on the front of many machines were hastily rewritten. Thus, 'Drop in your penny I will tell you true what Fortune has in store for you' became 'To tell your fortune I do not pretend, but I'll give you some fun if a penny you'll spend.' Henceforth such machines were strictly for 'amusement only' as far as manufacturer's claims were concerned, although as ever they went to great lengths to make the actual workings of the machines appear to be otherwise.

The success of such machines, apart from their novelty (they were to be made in a wide variety of shapes and forms) rested in the fact that however sceptical the public might appear to be, for many there lurked a residual belief that there was some truth in what they were told about themselves. This was evidenced in a 1939 Mass-Observation survey of women holidaymakers which revealed that 40% believed the cards they received from fortune telling machines. Flattery was the roller-coaster upon which these women were taken for a ride.

Occasionally, just occasionally, such beliefs were to have more sinister consequences as evidenced by a court case in Exeter in 1920, where an ex-soldier, William Fildew, was summoned by his wife for desertion. He had been discharged wounded in 1916, and they had lived happily until the middle of 1919. Whilst out with his wife one day, he decided to try his fortune on an automatic machine. He inserted a penny. The pointer spun, and stopped at 'Keep Watch'. From that time on he began to suspect his wife of infidelity and a short while later, whilst staying in Cardiff, he put a penny in a similar machine, again with the warning 'Keep Watch'. This was the last straw. He began sending his wife anonymous letters demanding that she 'confess all to her husband.' He even hired a private detective to follow her, but to no avail. Finally, unable to discover any details of her infidelity, and with the machine's warning still clear in his mind, he threw his wife and their three children out of the house! Of course, if we are to believe comic book endings, the machine had been absolutely right, it had warned him not about his wife's behaviour, but his own!

Edwards Coin Operated Phonograph, 1891.

160

CHAPTER ELEVEN
Music And Sound Machines

The production of music by mechanical means has a much older history than many would imagine. As early as the 3rd century B.C. Ctesibos of Alexandria had invented a water organ, or hydraulis, whereby the air of a wind instrument instead of being supplied by the player's lungs could henceforth be supplied by a machine. In spite of this early advance mankind had to wait, by and large, for a further 2 millenia before the fruition of so early a dream.

In the latter half of the 18th century, the Vallee de Joux in Switzerland (an important centre of the clock and watchmaking industries) was to witness the genesis of the mechanical music revolution. Early in 1796 Antoine Favre constructed a musical watch, powered by clockwork, and comprising of a comb consisting of a number of steel teeth tuned to scale and screwed onto the main body of the watch, the teeth being plucked by pins arranged on a brass cylinder. By the early years of the 19th century musical movements were being incorporated into a whole host of objects, most notably snuff boxes. In the course of a few years such boxes were to lose their original purpose and were to be manufactured solely as musical boxes. The first half of the 19th century was to see the establishment of an entire new industry devoted solely to the production of mechanical music, as a consequence of which, music boxes were to grow not only in size but also sophistication. From about 1850 onwards, what had hitherto been a home based industry (centered around the main watch and clockmaking areas of Switzerland and Germany) was to give place to the factory system, mass production meeting the increased demand for cheaper boxes with a larger selection of tunes.

The 1850s were also witness to another major innovation, the interchangeable cylinder which henceforth would bestow upon machines manufactured to accommodate such a system a virtually limitless repetoire. However, in spite of the sophistication and virtuosity which cylinder music boxes (in a myriad of guises) had attained by the late 1880s, the industry was to be knocked for six by the introduction of a new German invention — the disc music box. This was essentially the brainchild of Paul Lochmann and Ellis Parr, co-founders of the Symphonion Musikwerke of Leipzig. Interchangeability and ease of production were to be its key assets — a stamped metal disc was far easier and cheaper to make than a laboriously hand drilled and pinned cylinder. The 1890s were to be the peak years of disc music box production, confirming thereby the German hegemony of the automatic music market.

Yet, as we have noted, the late 19th century was to throw up a whole host of innovative wonders for the delectation and use of an enthralled populus. The year 1877 was to see the invention in the United States of the phonograph, by Thomas Alva Edison and John Kruesi. It was in effect the first ever device made by man capable of recording and reproducing natural sounds. As crude a device as the original version of the machine was (it was useless for recording music for instance) it was to elicit a

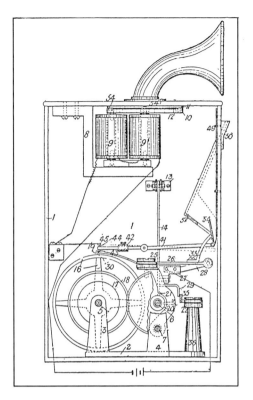

Top Left: Patent Drawing for 'Improvements in Apparatus for the Automatic Reproduction of Sounds from Records,' Charles Adams-Randall, London, 1888.

Top Right: Imperial Automatic Company, London, Advertisement, 1901.

Bottom Left: Henry Klein & Company, London, Advertisement, 1900.

rapturous response wherever it was demonstrated. However its development was to be a relatively slow process. Its impact upon daily life did not begin to be felt until a decade later, following the introduction of the hard wax composition cylinder which was far more durable than the tin foil sheet used on the original model. Synchronous to the introduction of the wax cylinder phonograph was the development of the disc playing gramophone by Emil Berliner. Although it was to take a further decade before coming to fruition, it was destined in the early years of the 20th century to sweep all before it, owing in the main to the cost effectiveness and relative ease of manufacture of disc records.

These then, in brief, were some of the key developments in the history of musical and sound reproduction in the last quarter of the 19th century.

The advent of the phonograph and gramophone during this period was to sound the death knell for the burgeoning mechanical music industry. However, the ultimate supremacy of the gramophone was not to be confirmed until the 1920s with the advent of yet more sophisticated technologies. Mechanical music machines were able to hold their own, particularly the more opulent or technically complex, because they were capable in the years prior to the outbreak of World War One of providing a much clearer and more audible rendering of the music they played. They could not of course compete in terms of vocalisation or singing.

The advent of coin freed machines in the last quarter of the 19th century was to play a key role in the marketing and popularisation of all types of musical device. Without the introduction of the coin freed principle many such devices would have proved either economically unfeasible to manufacture, or their development would have been severely retarded. The history of the early phonograph is a case in point, for in spite of its great novelty value in the late 1870s it was to be on the verge of economic extinction by the late 1880s. Until, that is, they began to be operated as coin freed machines in the early 1890s.

Just precisely when the first coin freed cylinder music boxes came into use has as yet to be determined. The British patent records are unfortunately not very helpful on this point, since the first coin freed music box patent was not granted until 1887, whereas evidence from other sources (most notably musical automatons) clearly implies an earlier date, sometime in the late 1870s or early 1880s. It is without doubt that they were to be amongst the earliest form of coin freed device encountered by the general public.

Once introduced, coin freed music machines in all their various guises were to become a mainstay of the automatics industry. Indeed many of the earliest manufacturing companies (most notably in Germany) of a wide variety of coin freed devices were to start out as manufacturers of mechanical music machines, turning increasingly to the manufacture of other forms of coin freed machine as the music box industry declined. Over the next three decades an extremely large variety of coin operated music machines were to be manufactured on both sides of the Atlantic, not only cylinder and disc music boxes, but also musical instruments of every kind as well as Orchestrions (which, as their name implies, sought to imitate the sound

With Disc Record

The Best Automatic Phonograph on the Market

At An Extremely Low Price

Plays 150 Pieces With 1 Needle. Only Coin Operated Phonograph in the World Using a 10-Inch Disc Record

Note especially that this machine is the *only coin-controlled* phonograph using a 10-in. Record, this making it possible for you to provide your patrons "with all the music of all the world." With our new specially pointed needles, the machine will play 150 pieces with only one needle. The records are not affected by moisture and can be changed instantly. It has a perfect reproducer and correct tone chamber. The quality and volume of the music equals that of much higher priced instruments.

The machine is operated by the ordinary electric lighting current, thus doing away with the annoyance of storage batteries. Our Price for this splendid machine is so low that it will surprise you. We carry a full line of records for these two machines. Write for list.

Fortune Teller Phonograph

Horn Attachment and Cylinder Record

A most attractive machine similar in appearance and construction to that described above, but bettered by the addition of the horn attachment, and the pennies dropped in by your patrons keeps the music going constantly. The machine thus, *without cost to you*, is an excellent substitute for an automatic piano, etc., and while providing your customers with amusement is earning money for you all the time. This machine can be equipped, if desired, with storage batteries for use where electric current cannot be obtained. These batteries will last a long time and can be renewed at small cost. Handsome framed sign and one 4 or 6-in. cylinder record free with machine.

Price, $60.00

| Width | 24 in. | Depth | 25 in. |
| Height | 69 in. | S. Wt. | 215 lbs. |

Price, $75.00

| Height | 69 in. | Depth | 19 in. |
| Width | 24 in. | Ship. Wgt. | 225 lbs. |

Mills Novelty Company, Chicago, 1912 Catalogue.

Automatic Phonograph

The New Slot Phonograph of Quality—Made Expressly for Amusement Parks and Pleasure Resorts

Will Stand Rough, Hard Usage

This new machine has been produced after years of experimenting, and in actual use has proven to be superior to all others.

It reproduces the tones of the human voice, band and orchestral music and instrumental solos with marvelous accuracy. It never fails to operate when penny is deposited. The mechanism is scientific, simple and durable and is especially designed to stand severe wear.

The improved record holder saves time, trouble and records; the large, well constructed spring motor is wound by an electric motor, insuring the steadiest known power and perfectly smooth operation.

This machine is not a "family phonograph" fixed with a slot device, but is especially constructed and the only phonograph made to operate exclusively by a coin and to withstand hard usage.

Direct or alternating electric current. When ordering always specify which is to be used.

Cabinet of selected quartered oak. Ornamental parts nickel-plated.

Dimensions: Width, 24 in. Depth, 19 in. Height of Cabinet, 46 in. Height with sign, 72 in. Weight, 150 lbs.

Fitted with direct or alternating motor.

Combination Phonograph and Picture Machine

A Decidedly New Novelty

Mechanically Perfect and Handsome in Appearance

This new illustrated song machine is a decided departure from the regular old-style slot Phonograph, and is admitted to be the finest device of its kind ever attempted. The construction is simple, and any one with an ordinary knowledge of machines would be able to do the adjusting which is required to keep the machine in perfect condition. There is a small adjusting device, which insures the appearance of the pictures at the proper time to correspond with the records.

The entire makeup of this apparatus is intended for severe public use, and is fully guaranteed in every detail of construction and mechanical workings.

Equipment: Rubber hearing tubes with ear cups. Slot opening for U. S. cent. Quartered oak cabinet; highly polished golden oak finish, with beveled French plate glass front exposing mechanism to view.

Improved Lens Holder allowing the lens to be removed, in a second's time, for cleaning purposes.

Large money box under separate lock; Sign, Record and Set of Views; Direct current Motor of 110 volts.

Options: Coin slot for any other coin than the U. S. cent, without extra charge. Alternating current 110 volts, 60 cycles. Spiral metal hearing tubes, in place of rubber, at $2.50 additional. Direct motor of any voltage up to 220, and alternating of same voltage in any number of cycles.

Dimensions: Height, with frame, 75 in.; without frame, 49 in.; Base, 18 x 24 in. Weight, net, 120 lbs.; Gross, 190 lbs. Packed in one case measuring 24 x 28 x 52 in.

Caille Brothers Company, Detroit, 1913 Catalogue.

produced by an orchestra).

Another primary use of music boxes was their coupling with a whole host of other coin freed devices in order to compliment them or to provide musical accompaniment. More significantly, music boxes were to be used as a legal ploy on gambling games in strict areas, whereby the operator could claim that the machine's prime function was a musical one — the playing of the game being merely a free subsidiary.

As we have noted, the earliest coin operated phonographs were to be marketed en masse in the early 1890s. The credit for the first such device has hitherto been given to Louis Glass, an operator of Edison phonographs on the Pacific coast of the United States, in November 1889. This however was not the case, for in July 1888 an English electrical engineer, Charles Adams Randall, patented The Automatic Pariophone — effectively the world's first coin operated phonograph.

However the application of the phonograph to coin freed devices predates even this. By August of the previous year two important pioneers of the early automatics industry W.S. Simpson and W.S. Oliver had patented phonographic appliances to be used in conjunction with other coin freed machines, which could by this means audibly advertise themselves, or indicate the user's weight or the amount of shock received. Indeed, the late 1880s and early 1890s was to see a vogue for such talking devices.

We can now turn our attention to the multiple selection machine, a device which was ultimately to become more familiarly known as the juke box.

Such devices are indeed much older than most would imagine. The early coin freed phonographs gave no selection. The user paid only to hear (by means of listening tubes) whatever cylinder happened to be loaded into the machine at that point in time. The opening of Phonograph Parlours in the 1890s (which as the name implies were shops devoted solely to the exploitation of phonographs) was to establish the principle of selectivity. In some, banks of coin freed phonographs were sited, each loaded with a different cylinder. Selectivity was achieved by means of the customer moving along the rows of machines and choosing between them.

Other establishments were to be run more on the principle of the music lending library. One such was the Salon du Phonographie in Paris. This consisted of two rows of desks and chairs, with a speaking tube and a pair of ear tubes attached to the top of each desk. The customer seated himself in the chair and ordered the selection he wanted by speaking into the tube. He would then deposit his coin, and the selected cylinder would be played on a phonograph by an assistant in the room below which was connected to the user's pair of ear tubes. By this means the customer had a choice of some 1500 cylinders.

The only selectivity a single site operator could offer was the periodic changing of the cylinder, which was to prove increasingly unpopular as the novelty value of such machines wore off. One solution adopted on coin freed gramophones at the turn of the century was to store a number of records in a compartment beneath the machine. The customer would choose

Symphonola: J. P. Seeburg Machine Corporation, Chicago, 1937.

S147 (The Trashcan): J. P. Seeburg Machine Corporation, Chicago, 1947.

Model A (Mother of Plastic): Automatic Musical Instruments Company, Michigan, 1946.

Model G80: Automatic Musical Instruments Company, Michigan, 1955.

a record, place it on the turntable, put the playing arm in position, wind up the mechanism, and then insert a coin thereby activating the machine — a fairly laborious process open to much abuse.

The solution to the problem of selectivity was successfully adopted by the hard pressed manufacturers of mechanical music machines. In 1898 for instance, the Regina Music Box Company of New Jersey marketed the Regina Corona, a large, coin operated, free standing, disc music box which offered an automatic selection of any one of twelve discs stored inside the machine. To quote a contemporary catalogue description: 'It raises at will any desired tune disc from the receptacle in which they are contained, places and adjusts it automatically and after having rendered it replaces it in its original position'. It is a description that sounds remarkably like that of a modern juke box. The audibility and clarity of such mechanical devices was to ensure that they were to hold their own against phonographic competition for a good number of years.

The early 1900s were to see the marketing of a number of multiple selection phonographs. One such was the Regina Automatic Reginaphone of 1905 which allowed the user to choose from a selection of six cylinders, and featured, in addition, a built in horn to amplify the sound. It was to remain in production in various versions until the early 1920s. Another, often referred to as the first true juke box, was the Automatic Entertainer manufactured by the Automatic Machine and Tool Company of Chicago in 1906. This was a selective disc playing gramophone contained within a large free standing cabinet. However the success of such coin freed devices (and there was to be a variety of such items produced on both sides of the Atlantic) was to be at best a nominal one. True success had to wait until after the technological breakthroughs of the mid to late 1920s, which saw the gradual introduction of efficient electrical recording and amplification systems.

The late 1920s were to see the marketing by a number of companies, particularly in the United States, of coin freed, multiple selection, electrically operated and amplified disc gramophones. A large proportion of these companies could trace their origins back to the heyday of the mechanical music machine. The names of the most successful of these were to become over the ensuing decades, household words, conjuring up all that was best in the juke box field, names such as AMI (Automatic Musical Instruments), Seeburg, Rockola, and Wurlitzer. The new found freedoms that electrical operation provided coupled with more sinister social and legal developments was to lead to a veritable golden age of juke box marketing and design which lasted from the late 1930s up until the early 1960s.

Before closing this all too brief a survey of the history of coin operated music and sound machines let us roll back the years to 1891, to a candid remark made by Thomas Alva Edison concerning his invention:

> Those companies who fail to take advantage of every opportunity of pushing the legitimate side of the business, relying only on the profits derived from the coin in the slot, will find too late that they have made a fatal mistake.

Oh how wrong Mr. Edison, how wrong!

EVERY
MAN
SHOULD
LEARN
TO
SHOOT !

Electric Rifle: Electric Rifle Company, London, 1901.

168

CHAPTER TWELVE

Shooting Games

> As for the shooting galleries, like the automatic shows they are
> everywhere. A few are attached to cutlers' shops; a few to barber's
> shops, where customers improve their marksmanship while they
> wait to be shaved; most of them however, are independent of such
> trade connections. The primitive type with rows of bottles for targets
> still survives, but the better equipped, thoroughly modernised
> gallery is more generally favoured and not infrequently flourishes
> under the special patronage of the local rifle association.

So wrote A. St. John Adcock about shooting galleries in turn of the century
London.

Shooting for reward or pleasure has its origins in the remote past. It was
to be the mainstay of country fairs for centuries. In 13th century England
every freedman was obliged by law to possess bows and arrows, and to
engage in regular practice shooting with his weapon on Sundays and
holidays. In the 16th century Bishop Latimer was to write:

> Men of England in times past, when they would exercise
> themselves. . .were wont to go abroad in the fields a-shooting, but
> now it is turned into glossing, gulling, and whoring within the
> house. The art of shooting hath been in times past much esteemed
> in this realm, it is a gift of God that He hath given us to excel all
> other nations withal, it hath been God's instrument whereby He
> hath given us many victories against our enemies.

In spite of Latimer's misgivings, the popularity of shooting as a public
pastime was to continue unabated. Most western cities could boast a
number of shooting ranges in their vicinity for the use of their citizens.
Many could additionally boast of shooting guilds or societies whose regular
meetings were always very well attended. By the 17th century many
shooting ranges had begun to incorporate moving targets, which often took
the form of running stags, deers, hares, or swans. The shooting range
therefore was one of the earliest forms of amusement to be encompassed
by the travelling showman. By the middle to late 19th century, as we have
seen, permanent shooting galleries were to be found in all major cities,
and, following the advent of automatic arcades, the live shooting range
was to remain a central feature of such establishments until well into the
20th century. That such attractions (by virtue of their use of real weapons,
and live ammunition) could be dangerous places is evidenced by a number
of 19th century press reports. In December 1883 the Daily Telegraph was

Electra Automatic Shooting Machine: Electra Company, Cologne, c1910 version.

Automatic Skill Shooter: Robbins & Co., London, 1894.

Automatic Shooting Range: Mechanical Trading Company, London c1895 version.

Running Hare: Original-Musikverke, Paul Lochmann, Zeulenroda, c1910 version.

170

to report a shooting accident at the World's Fair in Islington in which a man paid . . .

> . . . to shoot at some suspended bottles. The girl in attendance handed him a gun which he placed under his arm. He turned round to speak to the attendant and the trigger of the gun catching in his coat, the charge was exploded and the bullet, which was of small size, lodged in the girl's neck.

The police were called and the poor man was dragged off to the station, to be released sometime later after having convinced the police that it was an accident. Just a month later the Daily News was to report on another incident, in which a man was shot in the arm by someone practising at a shooting gallery. Mercifully, the advent of the coin operated shooting machine in the late 1880s was to help relieve some of this regular carnage.

The distinction for the first automatic shooter goes to the Englishman, William Reynolds. In 1887 he patented a coin freed rifle by which insertion of a coin into the stock would release the firing mechanism. The rifle, normal in all other respects, could be made to fire either live ammunition or pellets, by means of compressed air. It does not appear to have been very successful; no arrangement was specified for automatically supplying the ammunition indicating that an attendant was still necessary.

Much more successful was the machine patented by David Johnston in 1889. Effectively a distant cousin to the full scale shooting ranges, it was a relatively small countertop or pedestal mounted machine, whereby one inserted a coin into a cannon (at a later date into a pistol) and fired it at a target. If the coin entered the target an electric bell would ring and a delivery mechanism would be released, enabling the player to obtain a cigarette or some other article for his skill. In any other form it would be considered a gambling game, and it is really to this class or type of machine that one must look to find the first automatic payout games; since in practice chance, as much as skill, was to play a major part. As The Electra Automatic Shooting Machine it was to be manufactured in Germany in fairly large numbers for the next two decades and also throughout Europe (and possibly the United States — the International Mutoscope Reel Co's 1926 Shootoscope is evidently a late copy of it) under the aegis of the Electra Company.

Coin shooting pistol games were to enjoy a vogue throughout the 1890s (the Electra was to be the first of a number of different models). Many of the wall mounted gambling machines of the middle to late 1890s were to draw their inspiration directly from such devices, as evidenced by the names given to them (witness the Colonial Shooting Range and the Licensed Victuallers Shooting Range both made by the pioneering firm of Haydon and Urry in the late 1890s). In the gambling games, a trigger would be substituted for the gun and the player would attempt to fire the coin across the playfield into one of a series of pockets or compartments.

In the 1890s there were some very significant developments in the area of automatic shooting machines by as yet unsung pioneers of the automatics genre. The first of these was J.G. Cumming who was granted a whole string

Shooting Big Game: Automatic Sports Company, London, 1912.

The Marksman: Automatic Sports Company, London, 1912.

New Pistol Shooting Range: Nicole Freres, London, 1900.

of coin freed patents in the late Victorian era the most notable being that of 1893. A coin inserted into the machine fed three balls into a pistol, thereby enabling the player to fire them at a target and each successful shot dispensed the player an automatic reward of a coin or other article. Later that same year J. Robbins and F.T. Rushton patented a more novel version in which balls were fired at a row of miniature skittles, which would automatically reset each time a coin was inserted. Just a year later two more members of the Robbins clan, V. and E.C. Robbins, (they were to be based in Camberwell in South London and were to gain a reputation as laundry equipment manufacturers as well as manufacturers of automatic machines) were to patent yet another clever shooting game. It was marketed as the Automatic Skill Shooting Game and made use of a dummy pistol. No projectile was actually fired but instead hits would be registered by means of mechanical linkage situated in the base of the machine.

The next major innovation, and many will be surprised to learn just how early it came about, was the electric rifle, patented by J.L. McCullough in 1896. All automatic shooting games, (bar Reynolds' of 1887), were relatively small affairs which only mimicked the play action of the long established live shooting ranges. McCullough's machine was to attack the opposition head on. It made use of a full size specially adapted rifle, and a target which could be situated many feet away. It was much safer than its non automatic forebears in that it used no live ammunition. Indeed, as with the later Robbins machine, it fired no projectile at all. The machine was operated electrically and hits on the target were registered by means of a series of electrical contacts situated at the base of the rifle. It was to be an enormous success, particularly in its early years, and it remained in production up until the outbreak of World War Two. At least three companies were established in subsequent years to manufacture and market the machine, or versions of it. Yet having said all this, remarkably few of these machines seem to have survived the years.

Shooting games were to remain popular throughout the 20th century — witness the recent video game craze. Each new war or threat of war was to repeatedly see an upsurge in the popularity of such devices. As a consequence an extremely large variety were to be manufactured, one of the most popular in the first two decades of this century being the Running Hare machine. On present evidence it appears to have first been manufactured in Germany by the Original- Musikwerke Company of Paul Lochmann (co-inventor of the Symphonion) in 1906 or 7. It was a relatively small wall mounted machine in which the player attempted to shoot a moving hare or rabbit mounted on a rotating disc. A successful shot would reproduce the 'cry' of the animal as it was hit, and reward the player with a token for his efforts. It was to be widely copied in subsequent years by a number of manufacturers and was to remain in production until the 1920s. In its original version it was known as the Sankt Hubertus Schiess Automat (St. Hubert was the patron saint of hunters), although this title gave way in later versions to that of the Running Hare, in Britain, and the Tir Aux Lapins or La Chasse in France.

Other very popular shooting games of the period were to be made by

THE "KRAC SHOT"

MINIATURE SHOOTING RANGE.

Royal Letters Patents Nos. 11426 and 20838.

6
SHOTS
A
PENNY.

6
SHOTS
A
PENNY.

For Instruction and Amusement only.

AT the present time it is a difficult matter to obtain an Automatic Machine that is not liable to interference on the part of the Police on the claim of promoting gambling, and it becomes more difficult still to purchase a machine that provides bona fide amusement and returns a substantial profit to the owner with an undoubted sense of security. There is no other Automatic Machine that has the **expressed** approval of a **London Magistrate** as being perfectly **lawful**, and at the same time useful, insomuch as any instrument that induces men or youths to perfect their aim, and thus become familiar with the first principle of modern warfare, viz., "**Accuracy of Aim**," is worth encouraging.

This is the actual test of Magistrate Bros' summing up on September 3rd, 1902, at Clerkenwell Police Court, in a case when the Police, at defendant's request, had twelve machines of various kinds placed before Mr. Bros for his inspection—a dozen machines, and the Magistrate declared

the only one of them that was legal was the "KRAC SHOT."

The importance of this decision to Hotel Proprietors, Restaurant Keepers, and Confectioners cannot be over-estimated, as it assures them of the legality of using and owning such a Machine.

They not only provide amusement for customers, but, in addition, a handsome return on the capital laid out. In some cases **Machines have returned their cost to the Proprietor in Two Months**, and have never failed to provide **100 per cent. for the year**, and in many cases never once required attention of any kind.

Such a claim cannot be made for any other automatic machine on the market.

SPECIFICATION.

In polished, carved and ornamental satin walnut-wood case, with thick bent plate-glass front, lined with best green cloth, patent high-grade brass lock with duplicate keys. Lock up back for clearing money slot.

Measurement 21 in. by 19½ in. by 7½ in.

For fixing on Wall or Stand	...	....	....	....	£6 10s.
Ornamental Pedestal for same		....	...	....	£1 5s.

These Prices are for Cash on delivery and strictly NETT.

NOTE.—These Machines require practically no attention. There is no stock to put in same and nothing to pay for Cigars or other goods.

Kracshot: W. H. Ell & Company, London, 1901.

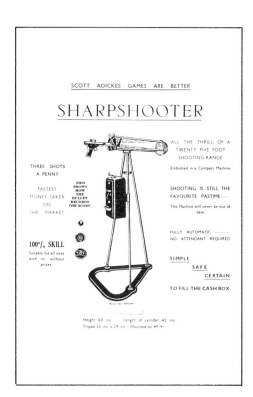

Left — Sharpshooter: Theo Bergman & Company, Hamburg, 1935.

Bottom Left — Rifle Range: Chas. Ahrens, London, 1934.

Bottom Right — Marksman Shooter: Chas. Ahrens, London, 1934.

the firm of W. Ell and Company in London, and were marketed as the Krac Shot and the Bottle Shooter. In America, beginning in 1925 with the A.B.T. Manufacturing Company's Target Skill Machine, shooting games were to enjoy a new lease of life. Although the Target Skill was based very much on earlier machines — it was a small countertop device in which a player fired five shots at a series of targets — it was to prove enormously popular.

In 1920 W.G. Patterson patented the first in an entirely new breed of shooting game, the light ray shooter. As with other machines no projectile was fired, only a beam of light which was aimed at a light sensitive target. Like the Electric Rifle it was a revolutionary idea, which once again allowed manufacturers to ape the full size shooting ranges. In spite of this it was surprisingly slow in taking off. The first light ray shooter was marketed in the United States in 1929 as the Radio Rifle, although it didn't effectively take off until after 1931 (perhaps the advent of the pintable at this time inhibited its acceptance). By the mid 1930s it was all the rage, with a number of companies producing different versions of it, some with an automatic payout.

The middle to late 1930s in particular were to witness a proliferation of shooting machines of all shapes and sizes on both sides of the Atlantic, a boom which was aided not only by social sentiments (which as we have noted in an earlier chapter were increasingly set against outright gambling machines), but also by world events. In this respect the 1930s vogue for shooting games was perhaps a subconscious limbering up on the part of society for the 'big one', which seemed even more inevitable as the decade drew to a close.

In post war America, the vogue for shooting games was to continue throughout the 1950s, helped no doubt by the icy blasts of the Cold War. This era too was to see the advent of a 'new' more sophisticated type of shooting game. It was pioneered by Eldon Dale of the Exhibit Supply Company in 1948 in the form of a free standing pistol shooter operating on exactly the same principle as the Electric Rifle of the late 1890s, although this fact was rarely acknowledged at the time. Later versions were to incorporate specially adapted .22 rifles complete with recoil and shooting sound.

A notable innovation came with a strategically placed mirror inside a cabinet which made the target appear to extend well beyond the depth of the cabinet.

Before closing this brief foray into the history of the automatic shooting game, special mention must be made of the Pussy Projectile Shooting Machine — perhaps the most popular shooting game in Britain in the 1930s. It was first marketed by the British American Novelty Company of London in 1931. It consisted of a large free-standing cabinet out of which projected a spring loaded pistol. Insertion of a coin released a predetermined number of steel balls which were automatically loaded into the pistol as the player took aim and fired at the targets. The targets, as the name of the machine suggests, were nothing more than an innocuous row of iron pussy cats. The player's objective was to see how many pussies he could shoot down. Had the targets been of men, perhaps a Devlish Hun or a Nasty Nip, then all would have been well and good. But this victim provoked far more serious moral questions — or so the R.S.P.C.A. thought. In 1936 they launched a formal complaint against the shooting of pussy cats! How positively outrageous! Luckily for all, Herr Hitler was to muscle in and save the day. Very soon, with the little pussies safely locked away for the duration of the war, Old Schickelgruber's face would be beaming out at the player from the back of the machine inviting him to knock his teeth out!

Smash Hitler Shooting Machine: British American Novelty Company, London, 1939.

Hercules Tug of War: W. H. Ell & Company, London, 1905 version.

Try Your Twist: Mechanical Trading Company, London, c1895 version.

Try Your Grip: Mechanical Trading Company, London, c1895 version.

Hercules Grip Test: Caille Brothers Company, Detroit, 1904.

CHAPTER THIRTEEN

Strength Testers

Devices for testing the strength of a person were in common usage on fairgrounds well before the coin freed versions came into existence. This is attested to by a corresondent of the World's Fair in the mid 1920s writing of his memories of the year 1872:

> Men with spirometers canvassed for customers to test the capacity of their lungs . . . hoarse men expatiated on the advantage of practising the manly and noble art of self defence by striking a pad attached to a painted figure of a smiling but manifestly ill used Chinaman.

The coin freed principle was to be applied to strength testers relatively early on in the history of automatic machines. That they proved very popular is attested to not only by the diversity of models manufactured in subsequent years, but also by their longevity, indeed, modern versions of such devices are still being made. What better way to impress your friends, or show your gal what you're really made of?

Today's arcade macho man has none other than Robert William Page to thank for the institution of this particular branch of the automatics genre. In 1885 Page was granted the first patent for a coin operated strength tester. As with many subsequent machines, it was in the form of a lifter. The intending player inserted his coin, stood upon an iron base plate with his feet apart, grabbed hold of a large handle with both hands and attempted to pull it up. The power of his lift was indicated by means of a pointer moving around a large dial. Simple enough as it was, it was to prove successful. Within less than a year J.S. Wallace (an important pioneer of vending machines) in a definitive patent proposed the use of a vending attachment for a range of coin freed devices, not only strength and lung testers but also weighing and electric shock machines, establishing the principle thereby that a player should receive some reward for his efforts.

1886 was the year in which Percival Everitt muscled in with his first strength testing patent, designed to indicate the force of a blow or punch. The player would insert a coin, and punch against a large leather covered pad protruding from the front of the machine. Again, a dial would indicate the force of the blow.

As with other areas of the automatics age, the late 1880s were to witness many more refinements of the macho-man's art. In 1887 the first patent specifically relating to a coin freed lung tester or spirometer was granted to R. Hewson and E. Crowe, in which a person was required to blow into a tube connected to a cylinder within the machine leading to a pressure gauge and dial. J.M. O'Kelly added further sophistication to the strength tester by patenting the first combination machine, which would indicate

Herculean Automatic Football: A. Barr, London, 1891.

Apollo Muscle Tester (Detail): Caille Brothers Company, Detroit, c1908.

Uncle Sam Grip Tester: Caille Brothers Company, Detroit, c1908.

Test Your Pull: P. Everitt, London, 1886.

not only the power of a person's lift, but also that of his forearm and grip. J.C. Sellers was granted the first patent for a speed testing machine. The player actually sat down on the contraption and cycled for all he was worth.

J. Conte applied for a patent (though he never bothered to take it out) for a new type of punching machine, much smaller than those which had gone before. This was designed in the shape of a negro's head which the patron was required to punch as heartily as he could. A successful blow would result in the delivery of a cigarette, to which was added a second one for good measure if the blow forced the pointer to the top of the scale. A later refinement of the same machine made the negro squeal each time he was punched! Novel as the machine may now seem, the white Victorian mind contemplated little upon the dreadful social consequences of such devices, and as a result they were to spend many oblivious years abusing, shooting, or generally knocking the hell out of effigies of negroes or other 'inferior' races.

The strength tester was to be one of the most zoomorphic or anthorpo-morphic areas of the automatics genre. Owing perhaps to the extreme simplicity of such devices much effort was to be expended in subsequent years in making the cases in which they were contained as novel as possible. One could grip against a model hand or an elephant's trunk, pull a tiger's or a donkey's tail, make a lion roar, or blow the hats off a series of heads, or make an acrobat perform. It was indeed an exceedingly diverse field which produced many attractive machines.

There were however two areas of the strength testing field which were relatively short lived. The first of these was the speed tester, which usually took the form of a bicycle. Relatively few such machines were made, and none seem to have survived the years. More popular perhaps were to be the non- automatic versions as evidenced by the following report from La Nature in 1897:

> One of the main attractions of this winter in Paris is the Cyclodrome invented by Monsier Guignard and recently opened at 14 Boulevard Montmartre. A bicycle placed on rollers is no longer a novelty since so many derive physical benefit from exercising on such a machine. But the cycle champions owe it to Monsieur Hurel, a Paris entrepreneur, that a genuine cycle race — including all the thrills and excitement of such an event — can now be held in complete safety, despite the most adverse weather conditions, on his indoor race-track.
>
> There are four contestants manning four cycles. The roller underneath the rear wheel of each of the machines is linked both to a measuring instrument which records the speed, as well as the distance covered and, in addition, to a miniature cycle with a midget rider moving on the replica of a cycle-racing track. The movements of the four tiny cycles on the track correspond exactly to the distance covered by the real cycles on the rollers, thus permitting the spectators to watch the progress of the contest as closely as on a real race course.

Left — Punching Machine: Rosenfield Manufacturing Company, New York, 1903.

Centre — Muscle Tester: Rosenfield Manufacturing Company, New York, 1903.

Right — Peerless Strength Tester: Rosenfield Manufacturing Company, New York, 1903.

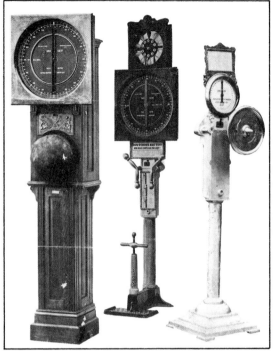

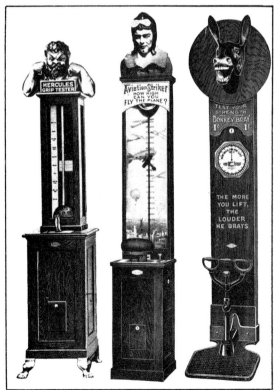

Left — Hercules Ball Grip: Exhibit Supply Company, Chicago, c1929.

Centre — Braying Jackass: Exhibit Supply Company, Chicago, c1929.

Right — Aviation Striker: Exhibit Supply Company, Chicago, c1929.

By the early years of the twentieth century the coin freed versions of such contraptions had all but disappeared from the scene. They were to arrive however, in a very different form, whereby a player turned a handle as fast as he could in an attempt to move a miniature figure along a mechanical track. This format was to effectively take such games out of the strength testing field and into another area of the automatics genre, that of the competitive game.

The second type of strength tester which was to have a relatively short lease of life was the lung tester. Although initially enormously popular, many different versions were made up until the early years of the 20th century, though it had one serious flaw — the threat it offered to public health. The fact that many different people were expected to blow down the same mouthpiece (some even took delight in spitting into it) obviously made such machines prime candidates for the spreading of disease. That the problem was realised early on is evidenced by an 1887 patent which made provision for a removable mouthpiece, a new one being supplied each time the machine was used. By and large such machines were to survive until the outbreak of the First World War, by which time the passing of public health legislation in different areas designed to prohibit the use of such devices, coupled with a particularly severe outbreak of influenza, put paid to the economic viability of such machines.

As stated earlier, the means adopted for testing a person's strength were exceedingly diverse. In all there were up to thirty different methods adopted including: gripping, squeezing, lifting, hugging, pushing, pulling, turning, twisting, blowing, punching, striking, and kicking. Of all these forms perhaps the most long lived is the punchball. Of the many different versions made, the most popular was undoubtedly that made by the Mills Novelty Company of Chicago, from 1903 onwards, which was to feature a fully automatic payout — the harder a player punched, the more money he received for his efforts. It was indeed in this field, and not the gaming field as many people imagine, that the Mills Novelty Company of Chicago were to achieve their first breakthrough on the international stage.

In July 1954 the following report appeared in the World's Fair:

> Hugh Farron, aged 24, whilst on holiday in Blackpool decided to test his strength on a penny punchball on the Central Promenade on Tuesday night. As a small group of people looked on, he rolled up his sleeves, stepped back a pace, and took a mighty swing. The next second Mr. Farron of Tyne Street, Bladon, County Durham was dancing about in pain whilst someone rang for an ambulance — he had misjudged his swing, missed the punchball, and smashed his fist into the strength indicator behind.

In 1959 a similar report appeared concerning a 14 year old youth at an Isle of Wight fairground on Bank Holiday weekend. He had hit the ball of a punching machine so hard that it rebounded violently and knocked him out! Though rarely reported, such events had been happening since the earliest days of the automatics revolution, proving that just occasionally machines were to have a will of their own. Tired perhaps of the daily pounding they received, they once in a while proved that they too were capable of giving as good as they got!

Mills Bag Puncher

Provide Amusement for your patrons and make money at the same time

A great big money maker that will last forever, is what operators have said about this machine. The player inserts his coin and is then enabled to pull bag down (See Cut) ready for striking. The bag when struck hits the platform above and registers the force of the blow on the large plain figured dial, and then locks and cannot be played until another coin is inserted.

The machine is a money maker because it will entertain a crowd, each one trying to register a better punch than the other. It can also be made more attractive by offering a prize each week for the one who is able to hit the hardest. This tends to stimulate the play.

Dimensions: Height, 82 inches; weight, 340 pounds.

Price, F. O. B. Chicago, **$100.00.**

Mills Owl Lifter

The "OWL" is, without question, the best money-making lifter built. Years of long and hard use have proven that the OWL LIFTER is built right. It will do all that can be desired and more. Attracts attention—induces play—gets the money.

Handles are adjustable to any height. Lifting force is registered in pounds on the beautifully colored dial. Deposit of coin releases locking device—release of lifting pressure immediately locks machine at end of each play.

Case is of highest quality hand polished oak, metal parts are oxidized. Base is well proportioned and of heavy cast iron.

The OWL Lifter has "made good." That has been proven. It will "make good" for you.

Height 67 inches, width 22 inches, depth 30 inches. Shipping weight, 150 lbs.

Price, F. O. B. Chicago, **$60.00.**

Lifting Machine took in $46.53 in thirty days. B. F. HIGHTOWNER, Pa.

Bag Puncher: Mills Novelty Company, Chicago, 1904.

Owl Lifter: Mills Novelty Company, Chicago, 1904.

CHAPTER FOURTEEN

Vending And Service Machines

The vending machine was in many ways the raison d'etre for coin freed automation, for by means of it a sale could be made or a service provided 24 hours a day, 7 days a week, from any number of locations, without the requisite overheads of maintaining expensive premises or hiring numerous assistants. Theoretically it was a godsend, the tangible realisation of every capitalist's dream. As such, it was to have perhaps more money and energy expended upon its development, production and exploitation than any other form of coin freed device. Its advent in the 1880s was expected by many to revolutionise society to an unprecedented degree, for almost all the commercial transactions of daily life could be seen to be within its scope. The possibilities seemed limitless, and like a many headed Hydra it was to seek a niche in almost every corner of society.

The 1883 Everitt postcard vendor was to be the catalyst for a movement which swept across the Western world heralding visions of a new, truly automatic age. Unhappily, it was a movement that in its greater vision was destined to fail. As simple as the procedure seemed — the insertion of a coin in a slot — the innate perversity of society was to make it ultimately an intractable one. This greater vision was to be bounded by the limitations of the very technology that had brought it into being. The early years of the 20th century were by and large to see the scope of this greater vision redefined. As expected it did indeed become an integral part of daily life, but on a much reduced level than had hitherto been envisaged.

Employees in almost all the retail, catering and service trades were at one time or another to feel themselves under threat from this new genre. The following is a list (though not exhaustive) of the areas of employment into which automatic machines intruded: the bookshop; the stationers; the confectioners; the ice cream parlour; the perfumier; the dairy; the hotel; the restaurant; the cafe; the public house; the post office; the bank; the solicitor; the chemist; the doctor; the matrimonial bureau; public transport on both land and sea; the garage; the lift attendant; the boot-black, and last but by no means least, the ever so humble lavatory attendant.

The initial impetus, as we have noted, was one which sought to replace many of the workers employed in these trades by machines. However, the intransigence of coin freed devices, which demanded perfection in all things, particularly on the part of the user, was to deny them the key role in society envisaged for them by their creators.

Having said this, the niches that the automatic machine found in society during the course of the 20th century were to be fairly considerable, particularly if one considers the numerous gas and electricity meters to be found even to this day in rented accommodation, as well as coin operated

Weighing Machine: E & T Fairbanks & Co., Vermont, c1890s. (Manufactured under Licence to P. Everitt)

Talkie Weigher: Chas. Ahrens, London, 1932.

1d Slot Automatic Weigher: Day & Millward, Birmingham, c1890s.

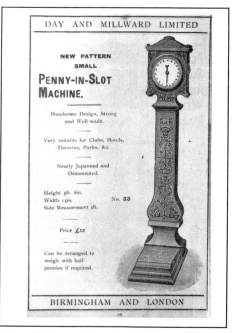

New Pattern Automatic Weigher: Day & Millward, Birmingham, c1900.

telephone kiosks, ticket machines, and even launderettes. In many other areas the coin operated vending or service machine was to complement the services or trades it sought to dispossess. It enabled shopkeepers for instance to sell low value items outside normal opening hours, or the sale of small items in locations where it would have been uneconomic to employ assistants.

For hoteliers, and places of public resort, it would enable the proprietor to elicit a few more coppers for services which would more often than not have been free of additional charge: electric fans, lights, heaters, radios, televisions, hairdriers, clocks, and even bed vibrators (whatever they were). Local authorities could recoup the costs of providing public conveniences by means of coin operated doors and toilet seats, or machines selling items as diverse as toilet paper, towels, soap, perfume, hair cream, prophylactics, and sanitary towels.

Of all the types of vending machine produced over the last century or so, the most commonly encountered were to be those which sold either cigarettes, matches, chewing gum, peanuts, or chocolate. No count has ever been made of the different models or versions marketed worldwide, but if such a count were ever possible it would surely run into the thousands. Of the wide variety of service machines manufactured over the years, then the one par excellence must surely have been the weighing machine. Although the first coin freed weighing machine was in use as early as the late 1870s, its full potential was not to be realised until after Percival Everitt had entered the field in 1884 with his first weighing machine patent. As with most of Everitt's inventions it was to be heavily marketed on an international level. Its subsequent success was to provide many people with their first glimpse of the automatics industry.

As with other areas, novelty was to play a major part in the success of many machines. Not only of function, but also of form. Although most vending machines were designed to look staid and business-like (particularly in latter years), a number were to take on the more exotic forms adopted by other classes of the automatics genre. As early as 1886 vending machines, primarily sweet vendors, were being made with the added attraction of a little animated figure, whose movements would be instrumental in the delivery of the desired object, with music sometimes added for good measure. More opulent were to be some of the machines of the following decade which were to be made in the case of certain chocolate vendors in the shape of a top hatted negro, or an elephant resplendent with a gilded howdah.

One of the most bizarre of these (unusually a model of the late '20s) was a sausage vendor in the shape of a pig you can guess which end the sausages came out of. Another of note was produced in the mid 1890s in the shape of a man with labelled drawers protuding from various parts of his anatomy. A coin inserted into the appropriate slot would release one of the little drawers, each of which would contain a different pill or potion appertaining to the part of the body in which it was situated. Unhappily, neither of these appear to have survived the years.

One of the most popular of all novelty vendors was undoubtedly the

Automatic Bar: Mills Novelty Company, Chicago, c1904.

Lady Perfume Sprayer: Mills Novelty Company, Chicago, c1905.

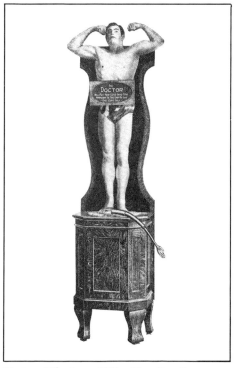

Doctor Vibrator: Mills Novelty Company, Chicago, c1910.

188

Clucking Hen machine, versions of which are still being made. First patented in 1894 it took the form of a life sized chicken sitting in a basket. Insertion of a coin would (in its earliest version) set a clockwork motor in motion, causing the chicken to cluck or crow loudly, whilst a little tin egg full of chocolates would emerge from an opening at the base of the machine. It was very successful, and was to be made in a number of different versions by various companies over the years.

There are two other classes of automatic machine which broadly fit into the category of vending or service machine, of which mention must be made. Both of them were to be relatively late introductions to the automatic scene: the crane, and the kiddie ride. The crane, of which many different versions were to be marketed in subsequent years, was first introduced in the United States in the early 1920s. It drew for its inspiration upon some of the earlier novelty vendors, which incorporated a little mannikin who, following the insertion of a coin, would shovel sweets or ball gum into a delivery chute.

The crane operated on much the same principle. Insertion of a coin would cause the crane arm to move across a tray loaded with sweets, gums, or other novelties (in later models the position of the crane arm could be controlled by the player). The jib would lower and pick up some of the sweets, which would then be dropped into a delivery chute. The vogue for cranes during the 1930s was enormous, not only in America but also in Europe where a number of manufacturers were to produce their version of it. Brasher operators of the period would substitute the sweets or novelties with goods of a much higher value (most of which would be glued down, or placed in unreachable positions). The primary function of the crane as a novelty vendor was therefore effectively subverted into that of a gambling game, the high prizes on offer, although in many instances unattainable, ensuring repeat play on the part of its adult user. Needless to say, these more blatant forms were to engender the wrath of the authorities against anti-gambling areas.

Far more innocuous was to be the kiddie ride, which as its name suggests, was designed as a novelty solely for the use of children. As a genre it still flourishes to this day, proving perennially popular with successive generations of infants. In spite of this, it was to be many years before it came into its own. It was originally introduced in the early 1930s in the form of a coin freed mechanical horse — the child sat on the horse, a coin was inserted and an electrical motor activated which imparted a rocking motion to the horse for a set period of time.

As novel as it was it appears to have been an unqualified commercial failure at the time of its first introduction. This was undoubtedly because there was so much else going on: gambling games, pintables, cranes and shooters all enjoying an immense vogue. The idea, after all, in the heady days of the 1930s was far too tame for its more macho contemporaries and appeared to have little mileage.

The same was not to be true however in the early 1950s when the idea of a coin freed kiddie ride was again mooted. The public climate, particularly in the States, was very different now, strictly puritanical and heavily against

Witches Cave: R. Reichert Automatenfabric, Dresden, 1930.

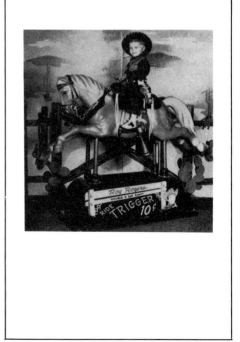

Digger: Buckley Manufacturing Company, Chicago, 1934.

Roy Rogers' Trigger: Exhibit Supply Company, Chicago, 1953.

190

anything that smacked of gambling. In post Johnsonian America the kiddie ride and the juke box were to flourish to an amazing degree. The kiddie ride was to be the star of the U.S. coin machine show, with at least ten different manufacturers exhibiting their version of it. Although initially only encountered in the form of a horse, the genre soon widened so that it encompassed almost every aspect of childhood fantasy. In our present age of mass production, when machines have a depressing tendency to look like clones, the coin operated kiddie ride is the one area left which still exhibits an astonishing degree of diversity of shape and form. As a consequence it is destined at some point in the future (when perhaps the techniques of fibreglass production have become an antiquated novelty) to attract collector interest.

However, our brief survey of the history of vending and service machines would not be complete without a look at the operators' conception of the 'ideal' machine. Such a device was heralded in a leading article in the 'Times' of February 1934:

> Now from the United States comes the machine which will stand no nonsense. Instead of suffering bad coins, or merely resisting passively by getting blocked up, this machine shouts manly abuse of the 'Stop Thief' type, and what is more comes up with its mallet and strikes a blow for business integrity aiming where the head of the offender is mechanically calculated to be. It does not stop there, it tips a bucket of water over the would be cheat, and last and best of all, it opens a trap door under his feet and swallows him up!

Stereo Card Views, c1950.

192

CHAPTER FIFTEEN

Viewers

The 19th century was witness to the birth and subsequent proliferation of one of the most important technological breakthroughs mankind has ever made: photography. Beginning in the 1820s, with the rudimentary efforts of Nicephore Niepce, and at a slightly later date, Louis Daguerre, it had by the late 1800s developed to an astonishing degree. So much so that by the early 1880s pioneers such as Eadweard Muybridge and Etienne Jules Marey were able to use exposures as short as 1/1000th of a second, as opposed to Niepce's original 8 hours!

Synchronous with the invention of photography was the advent of the stereoscope, thanks in the main to the pioneering efforts of Sir Charles Wheatstone, by means of which it was henceforth possible to simulate man's three dimensional perception of objects by means of two dimensional images. Although the earliest attempts had to rely on hand drawn images, the stereo photograph (essentially two photographs of the same object taken from different view points approximately 3 inches apart) was to prove the ideal medium. By the early 1850s stereoscopes had entered into commercial production and by the following decade were to be found in thousands of homes across Western Europe and North America.

By the time therefore that coin operated machines came to the fore in the mid 1880s, photography, and in particular the stereoscope, had become a regular feature in the daily life of countless affluent households. The year 1886 was to witness the patenting and marketing of the first coin freed stereo viewers. In November of that year, William Spiers Simpson was granted a patent for the first automatic stereo viewer. However the most successful of the early stereo viewers was that patented by a German, C Bach, in 1888 and marketed as the 'Kalloscope'. It was to remain in production until the early 1900s and was to be copied and plagiarised by a number of manufacturers. A coin inserted into the slot would release a shutter, and enable the user to see a predetermined number of views mounted on an endless chain. To change the card, the user pushed in a knob situated at the front of the small countertop machine. There being no time limiting device, the user was free to view each card as long as he wished. The Kalloscope made use of tissue cards (a development of the 1860s) whereby the image was printed onto tissue paper and hand coloured. Illumination was provided by means of a glazed apperture situated at the back of the machine. Night viewing would be facilitated by means of a paraffin lamp (or at a slightly later date an electric lamp) which could be clipped onto the back of the cabinet.

The Kalloscope was a great success, providing the public, for the first time, an intriguing insight into the wonders of this new three dimensional

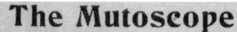

The Mutoscope

AUTOMATIC LIVING PICTURE MACHINE.

(1d. in Slot.)

THIS Machine is of the latest pattern throughout. It is designed for use in Hotels, Billiard Rooms, Arcades, Exhibitions, Stores, &c.; also very suitable for Piers and Promenades, being **specially constructed to stand out of doors.**

Complete with Stand & Reel

£5 0 0 EACH

Second-hand Machines only in stock at above price.

As a money Earner, this Machine is one of the best on the market.

Finished in Ornamental Colours to suit Customer's requirements.

The MUTOSCOPE is arranged on the penny-in-the-slot principle. The coin is placed in the slot, and the Picture is then entirely under the control of the operator, who can make it go fast or slow by turning the handle. When finished, the Electric Light automatically cuts off. The above illustration shows the Mutoscope with side door unlocked, and the picture reel in position. At the above reduced price, this is one of the **very cheapest lines** we have ever offered.

THE COIN OPERATING COMPANY,

11 Gothic Arcade, Birmingham.

Mutoscope: British Mutoscope & Biograph Company, London, 1898.

world. Coin operated stereo viewers were to proliferate over the ensuing decades and were in a large variety of shapes and sizes. In the main they used black and white stereo cards (which would occasionally be hand coloured) ss opposed to the more fragile tissue cards.

In the early 1890s clockwork motors were incorporated, so that the machines became entirely automatic, an additional benefit being that the time a person spent using the machine could henceforth be regulated, thereby providing the operator with a faster turnover. By the late 1890s and early 1900s some stereo viewers were being marketed as Illustrated Song Machines, which incorporated a musical box or a phonograph to act as an accompaniment to the pictures being viewed.

Another variation to be found at this time (beginning in the early 1890s) was the optical illusion machine which made use of a glass slide or slides to project an image by means of mirrors — much in the same way as the Pepper's Ghost illusion — so that it would appear for instance to be contained within a glass bottle. Although the vogue for such pieces came and went, that for the stereo viewer was to remain strong, so that although by the turn of the century the home stereoscope had become somewhat passe it was to survive well into the 20th century as part and parcel of the arcade scene. By the 1920s electrically operated stereo viewers came increasingly to the fore, dispensing with the need, on the operator's part, of winding the mechanism. In the 1950s 35mm colour transparencies were to replace the traditional stereo card in many of the newer models.

However, before dealing with the reasons for the popularity and amazing longevity of such machines, we should perhaps side-step a little and take a look at the history of yet another type of coin freed viewer. In 1824 Dr. P.M. Roget published his thesis concerning the physiological phenomenon of the persistence of vision; whereby the eye has the ability to retain an image momentarily after the image itself has gone. Roget's thesis was to be the cornerstone of a large number of optical toys which were to be marketed throughout the 19th century, beginning in 1826 with Dr. Paris' Thaumatrope, and culminating perhaps in Reynaud's Praxinoscope of 1877. Each of these parlour toys, by virtue of their use of the persistence of vision, were to be the direct precursors of the cinema. From the late 1870s to the late 1880s a number of attempts were made to animate photographs using the same principle, but few if any (although of great scientific curiosity) were to prove commercially viable.

However, the culmination of the efforts of these early pioneers was to come at a time when coin operated machines were coming increasingly to the fore and the earliest attempts at marketing these ideas was therefore done by means of this new medium. The history therefore of the early cinema is inextricably linked with that of the coin operated machine.

We have already paid homage in an earlier chapter to Edison and Dickson's Kinetoscope. Important as it was, it was not the first (as many now think) coin operated moving picture machine. The credit for this must go to the Austrian inventor Ottomar Anshutz who in 1887 constructed the Electrical Tachyscope. It would appear on present evidence that a coin operated version of the machine was marketed as early as 1889 (Anshutz

Autocosmoscope: L. V. Automatic Company Ltd, 1898.

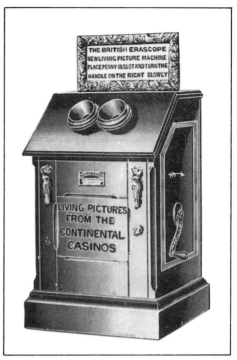

Erascope: Haydon & Urry Ltd., London, c1905.

Table Mutoscope: Bio-Automatics Ltd., London, c1905.

Mutoscope: International Mutoscope & Reel Company, New York, c1920-50.

was granted an British patent for such a device in 1892 under the aegis of the Electrical Wonder Company). It consisted in essence of a series of photographs of moving objects mounted on the periphery of a rotating disc, and viewed successively by flashes of light from an electrical discharge, rather like a stroboscope. Anshutz's pioneering efforts in this field were to greatly influence the development of the Kinetoscope, for instead of a rotating disc it used an endless loop of celluloid film some 50' in length. Although a great novelty at the time, and of immense importance to the history of the early cinema (it literally began with such coin operated devices) the vogue for such machines, which incorporated celluloid film, was to be relatively short lived; it was to prove a far too flimsy medium to stand up to constant usage. For a time at least.

The laurels for the most popular and most successful of all 'living' picture machines must go therefore to another type of machine, one which was far closer in spirit to the popular optical toys of the mid Victorian era: the Mutoscope. It was patented in America by Herman Cassler in 1895, the same year in which he and his three business associates — Harry Marvin, Elias Koopman (who was granted the British patent in 1898), and William K.L. Dickson (co- inventor of the Kinetoscope) — established the American Mutoscope Company. It was the first of such companies that they were to establish worldwide. In 1897, the year the machine was first marketed, the following description appeared in the New York Herald:

> The life picture by the mutoscope is pretty much like that seen in other scopes, except in the matter of pressing a button and letting the scope do the rest. You work your own passage in the mutoscope by simply turning a crank. If you are enthralled with any particular pose of any particular picture, you can stop the crank and study it. It is here that the mutoscope differs from its fellows in the pictorial machinery field.
>
> It is operated by hand and requires no motor, battery, or attendant; so simple it is that a child can operate it. . Photographic prints from a series of pictures . . . are mounted in consecutive order around a cylinder standing out like the leaves of a book.
>
> When the cylinder is slowly revolved the picture cards being held back by a stop, are allowed to snap past the eye one by one, as one thumbs the leaves of a book. An apparent moving picture is the result, and it is difficult to realise that the picture is not endowed with life.
>
> In operation of the mutoscope the spectator has the performance entirely under his own control by the turning of the crank. He may make the operation as quick or as slow as fancy dictates, or he may maintain the normal speed at which the original performance took place; and if he so elects the entertainment can be stopped by him at any point in the series and each separate picture inspected at leisure . . .

Much cheaper to produce, mechanically less complex, and more durable than either the Tachyscope or the Kinetoscope, its success was assured.

Regent Stereo-Viewer: Rosenfield Manufacturing Company, New York, 1903.

Vaudoscope Picture Machine: Rosenfield Manufacturing Company, New York, 1903.

Gallery Picture Machine: Coin Operating Company, Birmingham, 1928.

Stereo Picture Box: Bollands Amusement Machine Supply Company, London, 1937.

It was soon to become, bar vending machines, the most commonly encountered form of automatic machine and later versions are still occasionally found in operation.

The initial function of the various types of viewing machine apart from entertainment, was seen by many at the time as being primarily educative, as a pictorial supplement to current affairs, or as a way of seeing places and people one would not normally see in the course of one's daily life. However, these high expectations were to be gradually subverted as operators found that they could make more money by catering to the 'artistic' tastes of the public in general, and men in particular. Ladies in a state of deshabile were soon to become the mainstay of the viewer industry. Needless to say, such an emphasis was to lead from time to time to clashes with the more prurient forces of authority. Such incidents could at times verge on the ridiculous, for instance in a 1924 court case an operator found himself before the courts, charged with exhibiting obscene pictures. His crime? Showing reproductions of the paintings at the Royal Academy! Luckily, in this instance, good sense prevailed and the case was dismissed.

In closing, however, let us take note of how the more astute operator, whilst keeping well within the confines of the obscenity laws, would milk the situation for all it was worth. Witness this extract from a sub-committee's report to Dundee Council in 1926:

> Some of the titles displayed were: Girls from Paris; Naughty Bits; Mademoiselle from Armentieres; Don't tell what you see here; Very Frenchy; What a night; He asked for it and got it; Why men love women; What girls do; What all men should know; What happens in a -?; and 'It'. We objected to the titles and the proprietor has removed them, but now he has put up a notice which reads, 'Title objected to by the Town Council' so as to attract more attention. You can quite see that the connection between what is shown and the title is the objection. They are put there in order to excite the curiosity of the impure mind. It has been said that this does not matter, because if you look at the pictures there is nothing wrong. This situation is distinctly bad and not to be encouraged by the Town Council.

Just how wily the operator could be is instanced by the title 'He asked for it and got it.' The picture in question showed a woman baking a cake. A man entered the room and tried to kiss the woman, who thereupon turned round and hit him over the head with a rolling pin!

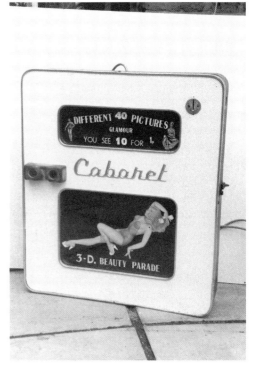

Nudist Colony: Bryan's Automatic Machine Works, Kegworth, 1936. (this machine housed a colony of live, NAKED ants!)

Cabaret: West Germany, 1959.

Peerless Pictures (Detail): Peerless Company, Canvey, 1950.

CHAPTER SIXTEEN

Wall Machines

The term 'wall machine' is a generative one applied to gambling games of primarily European origin, which as the name implies were designed to be mounted on a wall as opposed to a counter or the floor. It is a loose designation which applies equally to a multitude of different games, each of which could be encompassed within a wall mounted case. In its simplest form the wall machine is very closely related to the bagatelle game, the essential difference being the angle of the playfield which in the former is vertically rather than horizontally disposed. A large proportion of the earliest coin operated wall machines developed from the traditional 'drop case' games for long popular at fairgrounds. In the fairground version, one or more marbles would be purchased from the operator. The player would then drop a marble into an aperture at the top of the playfield, its course would be deflected by a series of pins until it landed into one of a row of numbered pockets. The number scored would determine whether or not a prize was given.

Coin operated gambling games were a relatively late addition to the automatic genre. Although such devices were to be spasmodically encountered in the late 1880s it was not until the early 1890s (almost a decade after the mass introduction of coin freed devices) that one was to witness determined efforts on the part of manufacturers on both sides of the Atlantic to market such devices. In this context the year 1892 was to be a very significant one, with the launching in the States of the Lighton Machine Company's Slot Machine, and in Britain of Frank Urry's Tivoli. Even the name of the latter was to belie its inheritance, since 'Three Marble Tivoli' was the name of traditional fairground drop case game. Both machines were to spawn a host of imitations and were to pioneer the principles of automatic payout gambling games. The Tivoli in particular was to be long lived, remaining in production possibly until the outbreak of World War Two.

In the United States the relaxed gaming laws were to lead inevitably to the development of high payout games. The vogue for drop case related games, although they were to survive in one form or another for a great many years, was to be relatively short lived. Emphasis in the middle to late 1890s was to be placed increasingly upon spinning dial or reel games. In Britain and many parts of Europe however, the overt chance nature of a spinning dial or reel was to inhibit developments in these areas. As a consequence drop case games (with their semblance of skill) and a host of sibling variants were to become the main form of gambling game encountered up until the middle to late 1920s.

One important area from which the early British and European gambling

Colonial Shooting Range: Haydon & Urry, London, 1899.

Pavillion: Automatic Skill Machines Company, London, 1901.

Improved Pickwick: Pessers & Moody, London, 1908.

Improved Pickwick: Pessers, Moody, Wraith & Gurr, London, 1914.

game manufacturers sought inspiration was the shooting game, which as we have seen had been incorporated with an automatic payout in the late 1880s. The Tivoli was similar to a shooting game in some respects in that the coin once inserted, would come to rest against a spring loaded plunger, and would then be fired to the top of the playfield. A more direct analogy was introduced in 1894 by Haydon and Urry known originally as the Game of Barrels, but later renamed as the Licensed Victuallers Automatic Shooting Range. In this the coin was fired over a series of four barrels, success or failure depending upon which barrel the coin fell into. In this type of game, of which many variations were to be marketed in the late 1890s and early 1900s, the gun of the shooting game was essentially replaced by a spring loaded plunger or trigger, or in a number of instances by the player's finger which would be used to strike the protruding tip of the coin in order to propel it across the playfield.

The year 1899 was to witness a significant development in the genre, for it marked a turning point, after which an ever increasing number of machines were to substitute one or more balls as projectiles in exchange for the player's coin. It must come as a surprise to many to learn just how relatively late such a basic development seems to have been implemented.

The next few years were to see a spate of innovatory machines, of which the most revolutionary of all was to be the Pickwick (a pun on the words 'pick quick' rather than the name of one of Charles Dicken's characters), patented by one of the great pioneers of the automatics industry, Henry John Gerard Pessers, in 1900. Its most important feature was its use of a moveable cup, by means of which a player attempted to catch the balls as they descended. It was indeed a revolutionary feature, one which not only made the game far more exciting to play, but which in future court actions would prove to be the mainstay of the defence in that they could argue with a certain degree of validity, that a skillful player would be more likely to win than an unskilled one. The influence of the Pickwick on European coin machine design was to be enormous, its manufacture was to be licensed by Pessers or plagiarised by a large number of companies. Legal action in the early to middle teens was to give it and a host of similar machines an added lease of life, versions of it remaining in production until the late 1920s. Indeed, most of the versions of it that have survived date, contrary to most collectors immaginations, from the early teens onwards rather than before.

In 1905 or so after, the budding German firm of Max Jentsch and Meerz of Leipzig introduced (under licence to Pessers) a new machine whose principle of play was similar to that of the Pickwick. This was the Clown, which like its predecessor was to enjoy an enormous vogue and was to be widely copied. If surviving machines are anything to go by, the Clown was to be made in even greater numbers than the Pickwick, and it was to remain in production in one quarter or another up until the middle to late 1930s. Indeed, post war versions of it were to be manufactured but these pale in comparison to the pre- war versions. The Clown, like the Pickwick, was to prove but the first in a whole family of similar devices

Heureka: Polyphon Musikwerke, Leipzig, 1900.

Clown: Jentsch & Meerz, Leipzig, 1913 version.

Motor Car Game (with electric shock): Pessers, Moody, Wraith & Gurr, London, 1924.

Airship Profit Sharer: Jentsch & Meerz, Leipzig, 1929.

which featured amongst other things, airships, airplanes, cars, boats, flags, people and animals.

The other type of wall machine that was to outstrip even these two highly successful machines, both in terms of quantities produced and varieties manufactured was that known as the Allwin. This consisted in its most popular format of a spiralling or circular runway along which a ball would be propelled by means of a trigger, culminating in a row of cups which consisted of two losing and five winning cups, the losers being situated on either end of the row. This made the machine seem a deceptively easy proposition on which to win, and in spite of the ball's perverse tendency to land in the end holes, was to beguile successive generations of players. The credit for the classic Allwin format belongs suitably enough to a German named Rudolf Walther, manager of the French branch of the New Polyphon Supply Company (the parent company of which was based in London, having been set up in the late 1890s with German capital). He was granted a patent for the ball release mechanism in 1913, and all subsequent official and indeed many unofficial versions were to quote this patent as a mark of their respectability. However, the basic layout, comprising of a ball fired by a spring loaded trigger around a circular track culminating in a series of marked compartments pre-dates the classic Allwin by a number of years. The year 1900 was to see the marketing of a newly manufactured wall machine known as the Heureka (the spelling is significant since other machines were made in subsequent years using the same name but different spellings). The Heureka was of German manufacture and possibly originated in the factories of the Polyphon Musikwerke of Leipzig. In terms of external design layout it appears on present evidence to have been the first of the plethora of Allwin related games that were to inundate Western Europe for well over half a century.

One common feature a number of wall machines of the World War One era was their use of multiple balls, whereby a player had to fill up a column or reserve in order to secure an award. It proved to be a very popular device both with players and operators alike. It was to be wonderfully amplified in 1931 with the introduction in Britain of the Challenger, patented and marketed by Leslie Bradley. This machine consisted of a series of columns which the player had to try to fill by dropping a succession of pennies into a coin entry at the top of the machine. A full column resulted in a payout comprising the contents of that particular column. It was to prove enormously popular, with its display of hard cash forever tantalisingly within reach, and it was to remain in production in a number of different versions up until the early 1970s. It too was to inspire a number of subsequent wall machine games.

The wall machine as a class was to be one of the mainstays of the automatics industry right up until the late 1960s when new laws and more sophisticated technologies were to oust it from its position of pre-eminence. Legally speaking, it was historically classed as a shady character, you knew it was up to no good but could never quite pinpoint what it was doing wrong. For the bulk of its history, particularly in Britain, it teetered on the limits of legality. The law differentiated between skill and chance, the

Roulette Visible: Bussoz, Paris, 1920.

Paris Courses: Bussoz, Paris, 1911.

Ben Hur: Caille Brothers Company, Detroit, 1908.

Little Stockbroker: G. Bradshaw, Birmingham, 1927.

machine in its many varied forms somehow managed to find the appropriate niche, having thereby a metaphorical foot in both camps — the conflicting decisions arrived at by British courts over the years were a testimony of this. Manufacturers, from the earliest years, kept payouts deliberately low. For the first 30 years or so of their existence payouts were primarily in the form of tokens or checks which could be exchanged for goods, or more illicitly, cash. Tokens of differing value would be loaded in the payout tubes at random, the odd one offering a return of up to 60-1, although this was relatively rare. For the bulk of machines an occasional 12-1 maximum payout was considered sufficient (that's 1/- for 1d staked). When the legal authorities became particularly touchy in the early to middle teens, token payouts in many machines were done away with. The more legitimate machines kept to the strictures of the new police rulings that a machine was legal only if it offered the player nothing more than his original stake. However, a coin return system, whilst keeping the police happy, did not please the player liked to fool himself that he was playing to win real money.

The more relaxed atmosphere of the late teens and early 20s was to see the reintroduction of the token system as well as the more liberal coin repeat, this latter system awarded the player his original coin as well as a free go on the machine, thereby offering him the prospect of bettering himself, if somewhat laboriously. This at least was the general rule, but as with all rules there were exceptions. Machines were manufactured that offered the player higher cash returns, some with variable payout. Another means adopted to allay legal objections was a payout in goods. As we have noted with the Tivoli of 1892 the player was offered an automatic reward of a cigar. Manufacturers, particularly from the mid 1920s onwards, were to reintroduce the system by offering either single cigarettes or packets of ten as the award (cigarettes being more popular by this time than cigars). Yet another payout permutation was the sweet payout which was to have its heyday from the mid 1950s to the late 60s.

From approximately 1930 onwards the dominant wall machine format was to be the Allwin or Allwin related games. The Allwin had by this date developed into a marvel of mechanical simplicity. Production costs as a consequence were relatively low. Skill, although arguably present, played an even smaller part in the eventual outcome of the game. As the one ball a penny game that it had become the Allwin could earn money for the operator at a much faster rate. Britain in particular in the 1950s and 60s was to witness the manufacture of a whole host of such games, each one fundamentally the same machine, but boasting a different design or playfield permutation.

As with many other areas of coin freed history, wall machines in Britain in the period immediately following the First World War were to undergo a curious metamorphosis. The authorities, as we have noted, became increasingly antagonistic towards them. For many operators, to succumb to the prevailing legal strictures would have been tantamount not only to an emasculation of their machines, but more importantly to their profits. A solution had to be found. But what? Why yes, of course . . . the electric shock machine! Why not give the customer an electric shock each time

Domino: Jentsch & Meerz, Leipzig, 1928 version.

he played on the machine? After all, the player wasn't really interested in gambling. (The operator was just giving him the opportunity to gain a little extra money out of the goodness of his heart.) What the player really craved was the electric shock . . . What dear reader, you don't believe it? Well neither (after some deliberation) did the British courts!

CHAPTER SEVENTEEN

The Working Model

Although automatons in one form or another were to be made in almost every century since the days of classical antiquity, the 18th century was to prove the point at which the art of the automaton maker reached fruition. This century was to witness many important pioneers of the automat: Henri de Vaucanson 1709-82); Piere Jaquet-Droz (1721-90) and his son Henri Louis (1752-91); the Maillardet brothers, Jaques Rudolph (1743-1828), Henri (1745-c1826), and Jean David (1748-1800). It was witness not only to the manufacture of their exquisite machines, but also to the establishment of exhibitions designed to exploit their money making potential. By the late 1700s (although almost all the leading figures of this period were either of Swiss or French extraction) London had become the centre for their marketing and exploitation.

From 1772 onwards, with the founding of Coxes Museum by James Cox, exhibitions or shows comprising wholly or in part of automata became a regular feature of London life, predating the automatic amusement arcade of the late Victorian era by more than a century — the crucial difference being that the proprietor or an attendant was required to take the public around the exhibition on a guided tour. As the new century progressed, such exhibitions grew not only in size but also in number; that of Signor Gagliardi (shown in 1836-7) consisted of approximately 200 different automatons.

By the 1860s these exhibitions were to be found not only in the major cities, but also from time to time, as part of a travelling fair. One such exhibition was described by a contemporary eye-witness as consisting . . .

> . . . entirely of machines that (the showman) had made himself with the help of an apprentice, and sometimes with the employment of a workman. The style of work would not be called high class engineering but there was a certain merit in every machine that it was a good working model. Besides two steam engines of different types there was a locomotive that carried a train round the show; a Jacquard loom, which wove silk ribbon with a small flower pattern; a diving bell in which two dressed dolls were seated, which came out of a tube of water after immersion quite dry, which was very incomprehensible to the country folk; the model of a steam-boat, which worked so far as to turn the paddles round under a sheet of glass which represented the surface of the water; an automatic doll which danced and said ma! ma!; an electrical machine which gave the audience shocks, and some other machines and mechanical devices.'

Necromancer (Detail): Canova Model Company, Birmingham, c1910.

210

We can see in such shows the embryonic form of the latter day amusement arcade.

In May 1875 the Leeds Times published the following report, relating to a current exhibition:

> Not a little interest is excited in this department by the many working models that are shown. For 1d dropped into a crevice like that of a tramway fare box, you may have soldiers on duty, and a host of other novelties. One of the men who shines here most is John Dennison, 26 Salop Street, Bank, Leeds. Mr. Dennison exhibits the model of a ship which is very beautifully executed, and which as the work of a man living in an inland town, reflects very great credit upon him.

Although John Dennison was not the first to fully automate a working model by means of a coin entry mechanism (he is predated in this respect by one or two other known makers), and he was certainly by no means the only maker of automatic machines in the late 1870s and early 1880s, he was nevertheless an extremely important figure in the history of the automatics genre, for he was essentially the earliest recorded person to make a living by means of the manufacture and operation of coin freed novelties, and was to remain actively involved in their exploitation and production from the mid 1870s until his death in 1924. From then on the business he had founded was carried on by his daughters until the outbreak of World WarTwo.

However, for all his pioneering spirit he failed to fully capitalise upon the enormous money earning potential of this new genre. This was to be left to men of much wider vision, such as Percival Everitt or Herbert Stephen Mills. Each of Dennison's machines (he concentrated solely on working models and fortune tellers) was hand built, and essentially a one off. None were ever sold until the daughters sold out the entire enterprise to the Blackpool Tower Company in 1944. Somewhere in the region of 30 Dennison machines are known to survive, covering a wide range of subjects, although unfortunately for us, the daughters embarked upon a policy in the late 1920s of revamping or rebuilding (and in some instances of even scrapping) them. Whilst this must have enhanced the family's revenue in the 1930s, the process effectively destroyed many of their father's creations; clockwork was substituted by electricity, original figures and subjects done away with, and new ones substituted. Whilst they managed to create some of the finest models of the 1930s they at the same time consigned to oblivion some of the most historic machines in the automatics genre. Only a very precious handful have escaped the net, surviving almost intact, complete with original clockwork motors, figures and subject matter.

As with all stories however, there is a curious twist. John Dennison's last surviving daughter, Florence, bequeathed a notebook to the Leeds Museum containing a photographic record of the revamping work they did, and listing the models made by their father. It was a wonderful, and in the

Drunkards Dream (Detail): Bollands Amusement Machine Supply Company, London, 1952.

The Haunted Churchyard (Detail): Bollands Amusement Machine Supply Company, London, 1952.

Midnight in the Haunted Churchyard (Detail): Alice & Evelyn Dennison, Leeds, 1933.

The Nightwatchman (Detail): Bollands Amusement Machine Supply Company, London, 1952.

annals of automatics history a rare gesture, where so much of value has been discarded or destroyed over the years. Having been left to a public archive it should have provided a useful and unique work of reference to future generations. I say 'should', because it has since been 'lost' either through negligence on the part of the curators, or as a result of blind avarice on the part of a so- called 'collector'.

However, in spite of John Dennison's relative importance to the history of the fledgling automatics industry, he was to prove, as the 1880s and 90s came and went, just one of literally dozens of makers of coin operated working models. As early as 1884 they could be bought over the counter at at least one of the leading London establishments specialising in mechanical music and automata; witness a Silber and Fleming catalogue of that year which features a coin operated mechanical Sleeping Beauty complete with musical accompaniment. Indeed, a number of the early manufacturers of coin freed devices during this period would make up models to special order. Few, if any, were to be produced in any quantity since almost all were made up as one offs and the subject range covered over the years was to be exceedingly diverse. Some of the prime users of working models during the last quarter of the 19th century were the various rail and steamship companies who saw in them a convenient means of advertising their wares. Witness this reminiscence from a 1935 article in the World's Fair:

> It is of interest that railways and coin slots have been closely allied over a very long period — most readers of more than 40 will recall when they implored their parents to drop a penny in the slot machine, which contained an exact replica of George Stephenson's Rocket. The earliest type I remember was mounted in a large glass case. Movements consisted chiefly of engine wheels revolving for a few moments and the illuminating of the case from the interior. Next, several of the big steamship companies saw the possibility of the coin slot on railway stations (not perhaps as a commercial proposition but a propaganda) with the result that at one time we saw a regular boom in "Ship Models" built to scale and mounted in large glass cases. Here again the movements and mechanical operations were of a simple nature usually comprising a slight rocking of the ship itself, and the lighting up of the vessel . . .

In spite of the fact that automata in general were universally popular throughout the latter half of the 19th century, and were to be found on sale as rich people's toys in all the major western cities, they were only ever to be truly adopted as a legitimate branch of the automatics industry in Britain. Here, they were to be manufactured as set piece scenes which had no other function than to entertain or amuse the user in return for his coin, and as such were to remain a mainstay of the amusement arcade business up until fairly recent times.

Because the manufacture of such machines was undertaken by relatively small concerns which concentrated upon variety as opposed to quantity,

The Belfry: Chas. Ahrens, London, 1930.

Chinese Juggler: London Automatic Machine Company, London, 1925.

Our Fire Fighters: Chas. Ahrens, London, 1930.

English Execution: Chas. Ahrens, London, 1930.

their documentary history has been poorly recorded. Since, they rarely if ever incorporated anything fundamentally new, almost nothing exists in the patents documents concerning them. In most instances they would have been made for specific undertakings and were therefore little advertised. Many would be made up to suit the client's or the manufacturer's own requirements (in which case he would also act as operator), and when their novelty had worn out (as in the case of the Dennisons machines) would have been discarded or revamped to portray new scenes or images. As a consequence, even the names of the makers of some of these machines have not survived the years, let alone a great many of their products. Of the names that we do know, the most notable were, apart from John Dennison: Nelson and Leonard Lee; Vincent Canova and Billy Thompson; Charles Ahrens; Frederick and Arthur Bolland; and Markie Kraft (both Bolland and Kraft were still making models as recently as the early 1960s). In particular, the machines made by Ahrens, Bolland, and Kraft came the closest to what may now be termed production pieces, in that they each marketed a fairly limited range of subjects, but manufactured relatively large numbers of each subject, their products being as a consequence well advertised.

Although, as we have already noted, working scale models of such things as trains, ships or pieces of machinery were marketed early on, they were easily surpassed in popularity by working models of a more entertaining nature which purported to depict scenes of daily life, either comic (such as the poor harassed father minding the screaming brats whilst mother lies in bed fast asleep) or tragic (such as the last moments of a dying child). Others had moral undertones, relating in the main to the evils of drink, or the inevitable brutal end of a life of crime; execution scenes were particularly popular, so too were scenes of a more macabre nature featuring ghosts and ghoulies and things that go whirr and clank for the insertion of a penny.

All in all, through the medium of these machines we are witness to the nightmarish world of our childhood dreams when all the toys come to life and re-enact the larger drama of our waking hours. What better way to conclude this brief survey of working models than this extract from a 'Punch' article of 1891 relating to machines on show at the Royal Naval Exhibition:

Before a Model Representing an Execution

A Daughter:	'But why won't you put a penny in this one Father?'
The Father (firmly):	'Because I don't approve of Capital Punishment, my dear'.
Daughter:	'Oh please father, please!'
Father:	'Well, let me see — yes, I can lend you one'. (He does, the penny is put in — nothing happens) 'Out of order, I suppose — scandalous! and nobody to speak to about it — most discreditable! Stop — what's this?' (A sort of woolly beat is audible inside the prison) 'That's the bell tolling — it's all right it's working!' (It works)
A Spectator;	'Very well done that was — but they 'urried it over

	a little too quick. I scarcely saw the man 'ung at all!'
His Companion:	'Put in another penny, and p'raps you'll see him cut down, old chap'.

Laughing Sailor: Modern Enterprises, London, 1950.

Cry Baby: Modern Enterprises, London, 1951.

American Execution (Detail): Canova Model Company, Birmingham, c1920.

Limehouse Nights — Midnight Raid on an Opium Den (Detail): Canova Model Company, Birmingham, c1910.

APPENDIX

Gambling, Cheating and the Nature of Play

'If of 'n' equally likely possibilities 'm' of these are favourable to the happening of a certain event, the probability of the event happening is m/n, and the probability of the event failing is (n-m)n.'

So runs the definition of a quantitative measure of probability, the principles of which were formulated by Gallileo, Pascal, Fermat and Newton. As with games of chance, the coin freed gambling game has its basis in Probability Theory, however to describe them solely as games of chance is to say the least misleading.

In practice a player can never be given an even chance of winning money, since a machine's primary function is to earn money for the operator. If a player were given an even chance it would mean no profit for the operator in the long run. A player must therefore always play at less than the correct odds (a rule which holds true for all forms of gambling), in effect paying the operator a percentage charge for the privilege of using the machine. Every machine is built with this minus expectation. However, Probability Theory holds true only during an indeterminate and unpredictable period of time, it does not hold true in the short term because of the basic principle that every chance event is absolutely independent from all preceding or following events. It still remains possible therefore for a player to experience winning streaks in spite of the minus expectation, although he will inevitably experience more losing than winning streaks because of it.

If however there were no limit set on a gambling game a player could inevitably win by doubling up his stake each time he loses, although in practice he would need vast amounts of money to achieve this. All gambling game operators ensure against this inherent risk by setting a maximum and a minimum limit on the size of the wager they accept. A coin freed machine automatically has these limitations built into it, therefore a winning or, more often, a losing player can never effectively double up or increase his stake. He can only make more bets and play longer. The more he plays the greater the chance that he will lose. The maximum betting limit, and the operator's percentage are therefore the two most important reasons why the coin freed gambling machine has been such a good business proposition.

Cheating

In spite of this, both manufacturers and operators have in the past sought to tilt the balance still further in their favour. Most pre-war three reel gambling machines attest to this practice through their use of the perverse 20 symbol, 10 stop system, which effectively ensured that a good proportion of the winning combinations were unobtainable. Most machines of this period had as a consequence a payout of less than 50%. This meant that for every 100 coins played into a machine only 50 would be returned, as opposed to the more liberal 70-90 coins returned by more recent machines. Such a miserly rate inevitably led to a rapid rate of loss. Operators also had the option of another ploy by means of a device known as a 'bug' (so called because of its shape). Screwed inside a machine over the selected cog, it would effectively stop one of the jackpot symbols from appearing on the win line. As mean as these schemes were, they were only part of a long chain of deception and counter deception perpetrated by all concerned. The player was by no means the least of these.

A coin freed gambling game ultimately needs only skill to cheat. The modern three reelers attest to this fact by their incorporation of a number of necessary devices to stop a player cheating. Inevitably, it was a process which began with the introduction of the earliest coin operated machines, many of which responded just as happily to a button or a good thumping as to a coin. The necessary refinements were to prove elusive for many years.

Players learnt very early on that they could use washers or steel rings to operate machines instead of coins. The problem was eventually solved by the use of a plunger which pressed against the centre of the coin when the mechanism was activated. The same solution applied to another ploy whereby a piece of wire with a loop on one end the size of the relevant coin was used in order to ensure repeated free plays. The habitual use of iron slugs was combated by the incorporation of a magnet which diverted the slug from the coin chute. The ploy of using a coin or disc tied to a piece of string, which like the looped wire could be used repeatedly, was combatted by the incorporation of a string cutter, or by redesigning the coin chute in order to make it impossible to withdraw a coin once it had been inserted. Manipulation of an operating handle by a player could in certain instances ensure a free play or a win. In response to this manufacturers designed machines so that the handle and mechanism remained unconnected until after the insertion of a coin. By the early 1930s the more sophisticated of the coin entry systems could test (and reject) a coin for size (thickness and diameter), weight, metallic content, and 'bounceability.'

In addition to all these ploys players of earlier times had more imaginative schemes at their disposal. One of the simplest of these entailed the use of a rubber tube which the player attached over the coin entry. A strong blow through the tube would be capable of tripping the mechanism on certain machines. More determined players could make use of strong electro magnets (having previously concealed the somewhat bulky batteries somewhere upon their person). These would be applied over the face of a metal dial or reel at the appropriate moment, thereby causing it to stop at the desired symbol.

This person is taking his 'profits'. His pencil points to the spot where the magnet was applied.

A more serious threat was posed by the 'spooners' and the 'tappers'. 'Spooners' were so called because of their habit of manipulating the handle of a teaspoon into the coin return opening of a machine in order to trip the paying mechanism. An alternative to this was the use of a watch spring. It would be inserted up into the payout cup in order to trip the payout slides. The answer invariably lay in resdesigning the machine so that it incorporated sharper interior angles thereby making any manipulation impossible. The other recurrent nightmare of the operator was the 'tapper' who by adept use of a ratchet gimlet would drill a small (almost imperceptible) hole into a machine, initially to be able to stop a reel or dial on a desired symbol. However, as cheating techniques became more refined, he would drill into the side of a machine, insert a wire into the hole, and thereby trip the payout slides. In many instances a whole series of machines could be emptied with the operator being none the wiser. The solution proved to be the incorporation of a drill proof sheet of steel into the fabric of the machine.

According to John Scarne, in his book on gambling, the most serious threat to the profitability of three reel machines came in the late 1940s with the 'rhythm method'. In support of this he estimates a figure of $700 million as the national slot machine revenue for the United States in 1948, stating that by 1949 it had dropped to some $200 million. This he states was entirely due to the 'rhythm' players, apparently paying scant regard to the increasingly stringent anti-gambling laws and the proposed Federal legislation against all forms of coin freed gambling games. However for all this, the 'rhythm method' (if it really worked) remains an interesting historical anomaly, in that its successful implementation required a very high degree of skill on the part of the player, by means of which he could ensure a successive series of wins.

The 'rhythm method' was developed following the discovery that on certain models of the period the three reels made exactly the same number of revolutions when the handle was pulled. It was also noted that the clock fan, which controlled the time the reels span, lasted on average some 7-8 seconds. If a person then memorised the relative positions of the symbols he could consequently judge where each symbol was in relation to the pay line just by looking at the 9 visible symbols. Then by timing himself with great precision, and before the clock gear went dead he could operate the machine and gradually work the desired symbol onto the pay line.

Once mastered the scheme was apparently so lucrative that a school was even set up in Las Vegas to teach it. It was run by a group known as the Rhythm Boys who charged fifty dollars for a complete course. In 1950 a pamphlet was published which gave details of the scheme at a cost of only five dollars. By this time a few thousand people were reputedly reaping rich rewards to the great chagrin of operators. However, as with all good things, it had to come to an end. In 1951 manufacturers rallied round and introduced a 'variator', a mechanical device designed to regulate the timing of the clock mechanism.

How effective the 'rhythm method' was at this point in time is hard to judge, coinciding as it did with a period of peak legislative activity. It could even conceivably have been a myth perpetrated by operators and manufacturers in order to enhance three reeler play at a time of declining revenue.

In spite of all the advances made in recent years in coin machine design, the irony lies in the fact that it is still possible for players to find ways of cheating machines, sometimes by the simplest means. This is instanced in a case reported in Britain a few summers ago, of players who had discovered that giving the coin slot on certain machines a drink of fizzy lemonade rewarded them with a payout of the entire contents of the machine. However, one last word of warning to any person inclined to cheat. Although you might now consider yourself the upholder of a great historical tradition, don't try it. It's illegal.

The Psychology Of Play

An axiom of economics states that no type of exchange which fails to yield mutual satisfaction can permanently endure. In respect of this and in the light of the undoubted success of coin freed gambling games, one has to ask what is the nature of the exchange that the machines propose? Evidently it cannot primarily be a financial one. In the long term a player will invariably sustain a loss, and yet in spite of the evidence of past experience will choose to play again. There are undoubtedly complex psychological factors involved, the least of which is the simplicity (on most machines) of the entire operation, which requires no skill or inherent ability on the part of the user, and therefore poses no threat. In this respect also, a player tends to see a machine as a neutral medium by means of which he comes face to face with 'luck'.

There are a number of popular misconceptions relating to luck and chance, not least of which is that they are inter-related. A player tends to play with a variety of half beliefs or mythologies in mind, believing that some force other than the machine is moulding his ability to win or lose. Probability Theory holds true only in the long run, but when applied to an individual in the short run it can seem magical. It is not possible to tell when, or how long those wins might occur. A person can be called lucky or unlucky and be said to possess a somewhat magical tendency for either. However, what a player often does is to mistake the tendency of luck as being real rather than apparent. Luck cannot be quantified.

Another factor affecting the psychological attitude of a player is the belief grandly referred to as the Doctrine of the Maturity of Chances, which arises from a misconception of the Law of Averages. A player tends to blind himself to the word 'averages' whilst at the same time remembering the word 'law', so that following a succession of losses a player convinces himself that he will shortly have a win because the Law states that his luck will change and that his losses will average out. In so doing he ignores a basic principle, that every chance event is absolutely independent of all preceding or following events. A machine actively encourages this belief by its tantalising display of potential winning symbols. Chance and Luck in fact belong to two entirely different categories, they have nothing in common, in fact they are in opposition.

Advertising and gambling game imagery have much the same purpose, that of making a person spend money, there is one major difference. The commodity a gambling game promises can never ultimately be fulfilled. Unlike the advert which might imply that a certain brand of aftershave will drive women wild (the buyer at least ends up with a bottle of aftershave), the player of the gambling game rarely ends up with anything tangible, even though a machine's image might consciously imply that he will. There is no bottle of aftershave for him. His nebulous reward is 'entertainment' or 'amusement' — that is, a momentary escape from the present for a glimpse of a potential future. In some respects this is attested to by the way players almost invariably choose to play back any winnings they receive, effectively choosing 'to live in hope'.

Incidentally, before passing from the theme of imagery, it would be of interest to note that it need not always be the product of a conscious mind. The symbols used on the reels of fruit machines are a case in point. The most enduring of the symbols used by Fey was that of the bell, which has appeared on many subsequent machines as the highest paying symbol. As defined by Circlot in his dictionary of symbols the bell 'is a symbol of creative power. Since it is in a hanging position it partakes of the mystic significance of all objects which are suspended between heaven and earth. It is related by its shape to the vault and consequently to the heavens.' When Mills came to redesign the machine he did away with all of Fey's symbols apart from the bell, and substituted images of fruit, so that they advertised the different flavours of chewing gum that the machine posed as selling. The ploy has long since lost its significance but the images persist. According to Circlot, the fruit as a symbol is the 'equivalent to the egg in traditional symbolism, for in the centre of the fruit is the seed which represents the Origin. It is a symbol of earthly desires.' One has therefore a curious combination, the collective image of fruit as a symbol of earthly desires, and the singular image of the bell, as a symbol of the heavens — materially manifested as money. It remains a curious though unconscious juxtaposition of imagery.

Roland Barthes writes, with regard to toys: 'All the toys one commonly sees are essentially a microcosm of the adult world; they are reduced copies of human objects . . .' In the same respect as the toy is the plaything of the child, so the gambling game or amusement machine is the toy of the adult. The images it uses are a microcosm of the capitalist world. It is a reduced copy of society, a society whose dictum is 'the power to spend money is the power to live.' The gambling game in particular parodies this dictum by enabling a player to be seen in a dual role, as a potential acquirer of wealth, and as a manifestor of wealth, in that he is seen by others to be giving up his money to the whims of chance.

The psychological need to play is inbuilt. Marshall McLuhan states that games in general are:

> a sort of artificial paradise . . . by which we interpret and complete the daily meaning of our lives. In games we devize a means of non specialised participation in the larger drama of our time.

KF

KEVIN FRANCIS
P U B L I S H I N G

$14.95 Paperback £7.95
$24.95 Hardback £14.00

£10.00
$15.00

£16.95
$24.95